Michael M. Dediu

World with One Country & its Ten Friendly Regions

Moving from 195 disagreeing countries, to just 1 country with 10 collaborating regions

DERC Publishing House

Tewksbury (Boston), Massachusetts, U. S. A.

Published and printed in the
United States of America
On the Great Seal of the United States are included:
E Pluribus Unum (Out of many, one)
Annuit Coeptis (He has approved of the undertakings)
Novus Ordo Seclorum (New order of the ages)

Library of Congress Control Number: 2019921120

Dediu, Michael M.

World with One Country & its Ten Friendly Regions
Moving from 195 disagreeing countries, to 1 country with 10 collaborating regions

ISBN-13: 978-1-950999-06-4

MSG0258583_p7TzR6somh294ofO77Lp
1-8400658091
1-3UXJ9C8
26MFD6Q9
1-3UXKV8N

Preface

For thousands of years the world was fragmentated in many usually hostile countries, which were all the time either at war, or preparing for war.

Now, finally, the big family of over 7.7 billions of people living on Earth want just one peaceful, free and prosperous country, with 10 simple and friendly administrative regions.

This book is exactly what we need to organize this beautiful country on Earth - let's call it Terra – with 10 unpretentious, free, collaborative and affluent organizational regions. There are clear and practical ideas, which will help the over 7.7 B people to have a **Harmonious World, with Sustainable Peace, Freedom, Health, Friendship and Prosperity.**

Michael M. Dediu, Ph. D.

Tewksbury (Boston), U. S. A., 30 December 2019

USA, New York (1624): The north-east side of Times Square, with the 7th Avenue on the right and Broadway on the left, and with Morgan Stanley building (1989, 209 m, 42 floors), on the west side of Broadway (left). On the south-east side of Times Square there is the Conde Nast Building (1996-1999, 264 m, 48-story office tower), and on the west side there is Marriott Marquis building (1985, 175 m, 56 floors above ground, 2 floors below ground, 3 m floor to floor height).

Table of Contents

France, Lyon, Place de la Comédie, l'Opéra National de Lyon (1831, 1993). The upper western façade of the Opéra has 8 statues out of the 9 Muses: Euterpe (music), Terpsichore (dance), Thalia (comedy), Erato (lyric poetry), Calliope (epic poetry), Polyhymnia (hymns), Melpomene (tragedy), Clio (history) and the missing Muse is Urania (astronomy). The Opéra maintains its own permanent orchestra, choir, ballet, technical, costume and scenery departments. Preparation for a production starts two years before the first night.

0 – World is a family of 7.7 billions of people

SUN: Yes, my dear Earth, you have this fantastic family of over 7.74 B, net growing every second by 2-3 children – well over 200,000/day, and over 82 M/year; the growing rate now is around 1.08% per year, and median age not even 30, just 29.8. What do they want?

EARTH: My good Sun, all they want is just one peaceful, free and prosperous country, let's call it Terra!

SUN: I see. This Terra is really big, total area over 509 M km^2, land area over 148 M km^2 – how you'll manage it?

Finland, Helsinki: a tall ship in the tourist harbor, in the south-east part of the city.

EARTH: Our friend – the author of this book – said that the people would like 10 simple and friendly regions called R0, R1,…, R9, which will be delimited (for easier administration) by meridians (or line of longitudes), with the assistance of the United Nations, each region having a pair of capitals (which will change every year), for example:

R0 between meridians 0 and 15^0 E, capitals: Bern and Libreville (Gabon)
R1: 15^0 E - 30^0 E, Warsaw (Poland) and Pretoria (South Africa)
R2: 30^0 E - 45^0 E, Moscow and Cairo
R3: 45^0 E - 75^0 E, Astana (Kazakhstan) and Karachi (Pakistan)
R4: 75^0 E - 85^0 E, New Delhi (India) and Tomsk (Russia)
R5: 85^0 E - 100^0 E, Krasnoyarsk (Russia), Urumqi (China)
R6: 100^0 E - 115^0 E, Jakarta (Indonesia) and Beijing
R7: 115^0 E - 180^0, Tokyo and Sydney (Australia)
R8: 180^0 - 70^0 W, Washington and Mexico City
R9: 70^0 W – 0, Halifax (Canada) and Brasilia

SUN: Very nice. Will the borders between these new regions be fixed?

EARTH: Oh, no! These are not even borders, these are just simple administrative delimitations, and all these delimitations between regions, as well as between sub-regions will be flexible – they will be changed after each census (5 years), for maintaining a balanced number of people in all regions (around 770 M) and sub-regions (around 77 M).

SUN: But in the proposal, which you present here, there are many big differences between the populations of different regions, and then between the populations of different sub-regions.

EARTH: You are absolutely right, but this is just the first implementation, which needs to be quickly put in place, and then, very easily, the delimitations will be moved a few kilometers east or west, to reach a balanced population.

SUN: Because all the people are in the same country, it is normal to modify a little its regions, for better administration.

EARTH: Exactly, and everybody will be happy!

1 - Region R0: 0-15E: Bern, Libreville, Oxford

SUN: Great! Let's see how this first region R0 looks like.

EARTH: Yes, therefore R0 is defined between meridians 0 and 15^0 E, with the first capitals: Bern (Switzerland), Libreville (Gabon), and Oxford (UK). For better quality and consistency of the management, we'll have the first two cities from the region R0, and the third city from outside. Actually, being inside the same country Terra, any city, sub-region or region can ask for advice or help from anybody.

Switzerland, Bern (1191), Berner Fachhochschhule Gesundheit Universität Bern, from Bühlstrasse (down, looking west), Murtenstrasse (left).

SUN: Very good idea. This first region R0 will have nice parts of central-west Europe (like the Alps) and central-west Africa (pristine beaches). Let's start with the meridian 0.

EARTH: All the meridians start at the North Pole and end at the South Pole. The meridian 0 passes through Arctic Ocean, North Sea, United Kingdom (a little west of Cambridge, then Greenwich, an east suburb of London), France(a little west of Le Havre and Le Mans), Spain (a little east of Valencia), Algeria (east of Oran), Mali (through Gao), Burkina Faso, Togo, Ghana (east of Accra), Atlantic Ocean, Southern Ocean, Antarctica.

UK, Greenwich: The meridian 0 (Prime meridian, 1851, official 1884, stainless steel strip under the man in red), Flamsteed House (1676, center up).

SUN: What about meridian 15^0 E?

EARTH: The meridian 15^0 E passes through Arctic Ocean, Norway (Island of Spitsbergen, Svalbard, Islands of Langøya, Austvågøy and Hinnøya, Island of Engeløya and the mainland), Sweden (for about 1111 km), Baltic Sea, Denmark (Island of Bornholm, for about 21 km), Baltic Sea, Poland, Germany (For about 16 km near Görlitz), Czech Republic, Austria, Slovenia, Croatia, Adriatic Sea, Italy (On the beach of Termoli, Tyrrhenian Sea, Island of Vulcano, Island of Sicily, across the Etna volcano), Mediterranean Sea, Libya, Chad (first 1 km, second Lake Chad, west of N'Djamena), Niger, Cameroon, Central African Republic, Republic of the Congo, Democratic Republic of the Congo, Angola, Namibia, Atlantic Ocean, Southern Ocean, Antarctica (Queen Maud Land).

UK, Oxford: On Oriel Street, looking southeast to the west façade of Oriel College (1326), Merton St, Corpus Christy College (1517, right).

SUN: Let's see what capitals we have in R0.

EARTH: We have plenty of capitals in R0: Algiers of Algeria, Andorra la Vella of Andorra, Luanda of Angola, Brussels of Belgium, Poro-Novo of Benin, Ouagadougou of Burkina Faso, Yaounde of Cameroon, N'Djamena of Chad, Yamoussoukro of Cote d'Ivoire, Prague of Czech Republic, Copenhagen of Denmark, Malabo of Equatorial Guinea, Torshavn of Faroe Islands, Paris of France, Libreville of Gabon, Berlin of Germany, St. Peter Port of Guernsey, Conakry of Guinea, Rome of Italy, Monrovia of Liberia, Tripoli of Libya, Vaduz of Liechtenstein, Luxembourg of Luxembourg, Bamako of Mali, Valletta of Malta, The Hague of Netherlands, Niamey of Niger, Abuja of Nigeria, Oslo of Norway, Lisbon of Portugal, San Marino of San Marino, Sao Tome of Sao Tome and Principe, Freetown of Sierra Leone, Ljubljana of Slovenia, Madrid of Spain, Bern of Switzerland, Lome of Togo, Tunis of Tunisia, and Vatican City of Vatican.

In Malmö, southwest of Sweden, taking the boat from Malmö to Köpenhamn (Copenhagen, Denmark, 25 km northwest of Malmö).

Sub-Region R00-1E: Paris, Niamey, Magdeburg

SUN: Therefore, it is really easy to form the 10 superb sub-regions R00 to R09

EARTH: Yes indeed, the sub-region R00 will have the capitals Paris (France), Niamey (Niger), and Magdeburg (Germany).
This sub-region R00 is around the meridian (longitude) 0.75^0 E $(0 - 1.5^0$ E), having small areas from the Arctic Ocean, Atlantic Ocean, United Kingdom, France, Spain, Algeria, Mali, Niger, Burkina Faso, Benin, Togo, Ghana, Southern Ocean, and Antarctica.

France, Paris: L'Arc de Triomphe de l'Étoile (1836, 50 m), in the center of the Place Charles de Gaulle (1890-1970), seen from Champs-Élysées.

Sub-Region R01-2E: Brussels, Porto-Novo, Toronto.

SUN: And the wonderful R01?

EARTH: The sub-region R01 will have the capitals Brussels (Belgium), Porto-Novo (Benin), and Toronto (Canada).
This sub-region R01 is around the meridian (longitude) 2.25^0 E (1.5^0 E – 3^0 E), having small areas from the Arctic Ocean, Atlantic Ocean, Belgium, France, Spain, Algeria, Mali, Niger, Benin, Nigeria, Southern Ocean, and Antarctica.

Canada: interior of Toronto Pearson International Airport (1984, 22 km northwest of downtown Toronto, in Mississauga, Ontario).

Sub-Region R02-4E: Amsterdam, Algiers, Graz

SUN: Let's see the great R02.

EARTH: The sub-region R02 will have the capitals Amsterdam (Netherlands), Algiers (Algeria), and Graz (Austria). This sub-region R02 is around the meridian (longitude) 3.75^0 E (3^0 E $- 4.5^0$ E), having small areas from the Arctic Ocean, Atlantic Ocean, Netherlands, Belgium, France, Spain, Algeria, Mali, Niger, Nigeria, Southern Ocean, and Antarctica.

Boston Harbor (1614): Rowes Wharf (1666, 1764, 1987): the stern (rear) of Clipper Stad Amsterdam (2000, 76 m x 10.5 m x 4.8 m x 46.5 m) moored here, with the poop deck clearly visible.

Sub-Region R03-5E: Luxembourg, Sao Tome, Adelaide

SUN: We are now at the remarkable R03.

EARTH: The sub-region R03 will have the capitals Luxembourg (Luxembourg), Sao Tome (Sao Tome and Principe), and Adelaide (Australia).

This sub-region R03 is around the meridian (longitude) 5.25^0 E (4.5^0 E – 6^0 E), having small areas from the Arctic Ocean, Atlantic Ocean, Norway, Netherlands, Belgium, France, Algeria, Niger, Nigeria, Southern Ocean, and Antarctica.

Australia: Sydney Harbour National Park – Dobroyd Head (600 m east of Crater cove lookout), looking south to Gubbuh (right center) and Hornby Lighthouse (center back).

Sub-Region R04-7E: Abuja, Bochum, Nikko

SUN: Let's see now the amazing R04.

EARTH: The sub-region R04 will have the capitals of Abuja (Nigeria), Bochum (Germany), and Nikko (Japan).
This sub-region R04 is around the meridian (longitude) 6.75^0 E (6^0 E $-$ 7.5^0 E), having small areas from the Arctic Ocean, Atlantic Ocean, Norway, Germany, Netherlands, France, Switzerland, Italy, Algeria, Niger, Nigeria, Southern Ocean, and Antarctica.

Japan, Nikko (140 km north of Tokyo): Honden (1619, the main building enshrining the three deities of the Futarasan shrine).

Sub-Region R05-8E: Malabo, Zürich, Leeds

SUN: The astonishing R05 is the next.

EARTH: The sub-region R05 will have the capitals of Malabo (Equatorial Guinea), Zürich (Switzerland), and Leeds (UK). This sub-region R05 is around the meridian (longitude) 8.25^0 E (7.5^0 E – 9^0 E), having small areas from the Arctic Ocean, Atlantic Ocean, Norway, Germany, France, Switzerland, Italy, Algeria, Tunisia, Niger, Nigeria, Southern Ocean, and Antarctica.

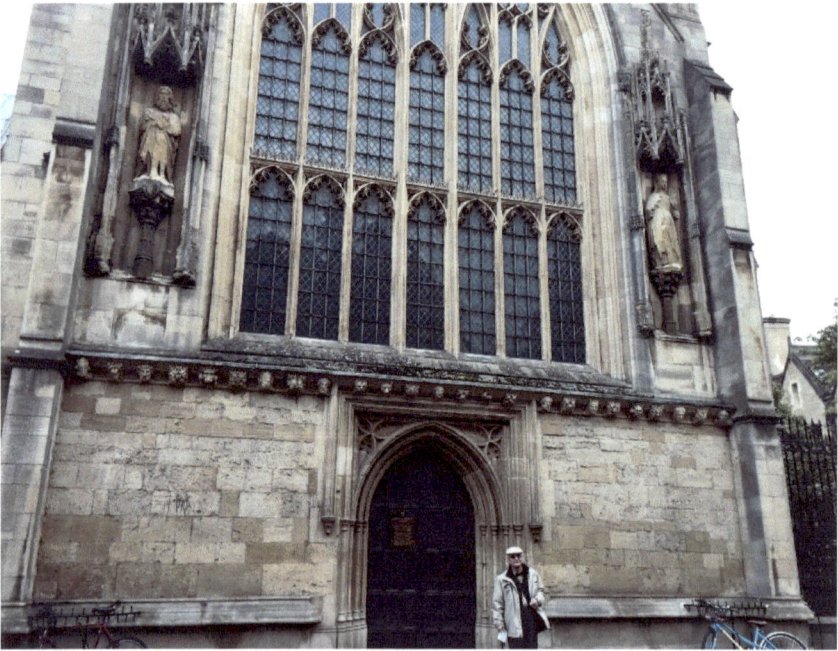

UK, Oxford: From Merton Street, looking south to the west part of the north facade of Merton College Chapel (1294).

Sub-Region R06-10E: Oslo, Tunis, Sheffield

SUN: Now the surprising R06.

EARTH: The sub-region R06 will have the capitals of Oslo (Norway), Tunis (Tunisia), and Sheffield (UK).
This sub-region R06 is around the meridian (longitude) 9.75^0 E (9^0 E – 10.5^0 E), having small areas from the Arctic Ocean, Norway, Denmark, Germany, Austria, Switzerland, Italy, Tunisia, Libya, Algeria, Niger, Nigeria, Cameroon, Equatorial Guinea, Gabon, Atlantic Ocean, Southern Ocean, and Antarctica.

UK, Cambridge: On Trumpington St, looking southeast, near Corpus Christi College (right back, 1352, the sixth in the University of Cambridge's history)

Sub-Region R07-11E: Roma, Luanda, Yamagata

SUN: Let's see the astounding R07.

EARTH: The sub-region R07 will have the capitals of Roma (Italy), Luanda (Angola), and Yamagata (Japan).
This sub-region R07 is around the meridian (longitude) 11.25^0 E (10.5^0 E – 12^0 E), having small areas from the Arctic Ocean, Norway, Sweden, Denmark, Germany, Austria, Italy, Libya, Niger, Nigeria, Cameroon, Gabon, Republic of the Congo, Angola, Namibia, Atlantic Ocean, Southern Ocean, and Antarctica.

Italy, Roma, Forum Romanum (80 BC, right), Temple of Saturn 42 BC, center, Arch of Severus 203, center-left, Temple of Vespasian 80, left.

Sub-Region R08-13E: Berlin, Tripoli, New York

SUN: It is now the amazing R08.

EARTH: The sub-region R08 will have the capitals in Berlin (Germany), Tripoli (Libya), and New York (USA).
This sub-region R08 is around the meridian (longitude) 12.75^0 E $(12^0$ E $- 13.5^0$ E), having small areas from the Arctic Ocean, Norway, Sweden, Germany, Czech Republic, Austria, Italy, Libya, Niger, Nigeria, Cameroon, Gabon, Republic of the Congo, Angola, Democratic Republic of the Congo, Namibia, Atlantic Ocean, Southern Ocean, and Antarctica.

USA, New York, April 1994, Saks & Company (back) on Vesey Street, 200 m northeast of the north tower of the World Trade Center.

Sub-Region R09-14E: Prague, N'Djamena, Brisbane

SUN: And the unbeatable 10th sub-region R09.

EARTH: The sub-region R09 will have the capitals of Prague (Czech Republic), N'Djamena (Chad), and Brisbane (Australia).

This sub-region R09 is around the meridian (longitude) 14.25^0 E (13.5^0 E – 15^0 E), having small areas from the Arctic Ocean, Norway, Sweden, Germany, Czech Republic, Austria, Slovenia, Croatia, Italy, Libya, Niger, Chad, Nigeria, Cameroon, Gabon, Republic of the Congo, Democratic Republic of the Congo, Angola, Namibia, Atlantic Ocean, Southern Ocean, and Antarctica.

Australia: Looking southeast to the northwest side of the Sydney Opera House

2 - Region R1: 15E-30E: Warsaw, Pretoria, Miami

SUN: The previous Region R0 and its 10 sub-regions are great! Let's see now the second magnificent region R1.

EARTH: Yes, R1 is defined between meridians 15^0 E and 30^0 E, with the first capitals in Warsaw (Poland), Pretoria (South Africa), and Miami (FL, USA).

SUN: This second region R1 has more land than the first region R0, and contains parts of the center-east Europe and center-east Africa. We know the meridian 15^0 E, let's see know the meridian 30^0 E.

EARTH: The meridian 30^0 E is from the North Pole across the Arctic Ocean, Europe, Turkey, Africa, the Indian Ocean, the Southern Ocean, and Antarctica to the South Pole. More precisely, it passes through the Arctic Ocean, just west of Kirkenes, Norway, Russia, Finland, Russia (just west of Saint Petersburg), Belarus, Ukraine, Moldova (12 km), Ukraine, Black Sea, Turkey, Mediterranean Sea, Egypt, Sudan, South Sudan, Democratic Republic of the Congo, Uganda, Rwanda (just west of Kigali), Burundi, Tanzania, Lake Tanganyika, Democratic Republic of the Congo, Zambia, Zimbabwe, South Africa (Limpopo, Eastern Cape), Indian Ocean, Southern Ocean, and Antarctica (Queen Maud Land).

USA, Newport (1639), Chateau-sur-Mer, 1851, 17 acres, William Shepard Wetmore (1801-1862, a merchant in the China trade).

USA: 3 Dec 2009, from Avenue Louis Pasteur (1822-1895, French microbiologist), Boston Public Latin School (1635, Schola Latina Bostoniensis, the oldest and the first public exam school in the US).

Sub-Region R10-16E: Zagreb, Brazzaville, Nantes

SUN: Very nice, let's start now with the first if its 10 sub-regions, the glorious R10.

EARTH: Yes, the sub-region R10 will have the capitals in Zagreb (Croatia), Brazzaville (Congo), and Nantes (France). This sub-region R10 is around the meridian (longitude) 15.75^0 E (15^0 E – 16.5^0 E), having small areas from the Arctic Ocean, Norway, Sweden, Poland, Czech Republic, Austria, Slovenia, Croatia, Bosnia and Herzegovina, Italy, Libya, Chad, Central African Republic, Cameroon, Gabon, Republic of the Congo, Democratic Republic of the Congo, Angola, Namibia, Atlantic Ocean, Southern Ocean, and Antarctica.

France, Paris (250 BC): l'Hôtel de Ville (City Hall since 1357, King Francis I started this building in 1533, finished 1628, 1873-1892.

Sub-Region R11-17E: Vienna, Windhoek, Bilbao

SUN: Now the brilliant sub-region R11.

EARTH: The sub-region R11 will have the capitals in Vienna (Austria), Windhoek (Namibia), and Bilbao (Spain).
This sub-region R11 is around the meridian (longitude) 17.25^0 E $(16.5^0$ E $- 18^0$ E), having small areas from the Arctic Ocean, Norway, Sweden, Poland, Czech Republic, Slovakia, Austria, Hungary, Croatia, Bosnia and Herzegovina, Italy, Libya, Chad, Central African Republic, Republic of the Congo, Democratic Republic of the Congo, Angola, Namibia, South Africa, Atlantic Ocean, Southern Ocean, and Antarctica.

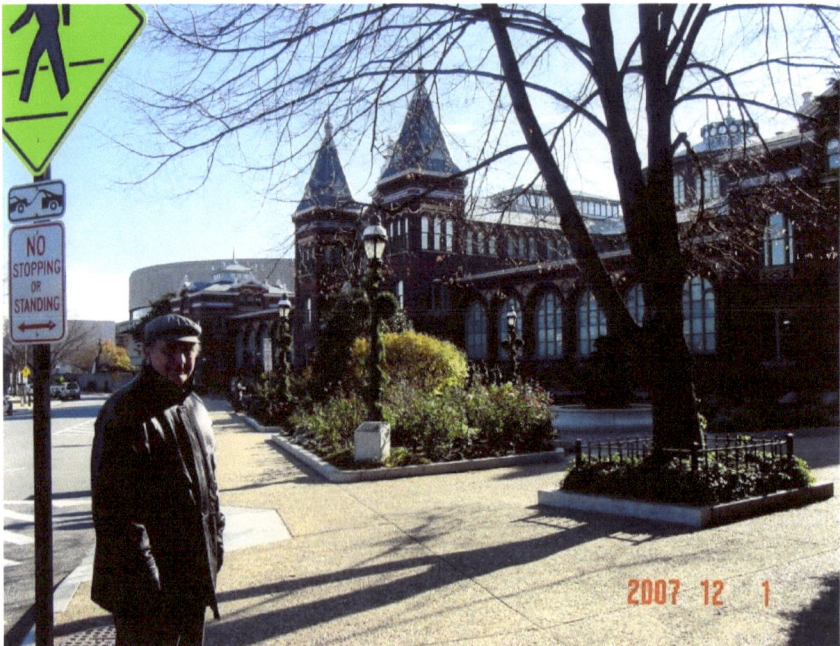

Washington, DC (1790): the Smithsonian Institution Building (1849-1855) on Jefferson Drive SW, in the National Mall.

Sub-Region R12-19E: Stockholm, Bangui, Florence

SUN: The dazzling R12 comes next.

EARTH: The sub-region R12 will have the capitals in Stockholm (Sweden), Bangui (Central African Republic), and Florence (Italy).

This sub-region R12 is around the meridian (longitude) 18.75^0 E (18^0 E – 19.5^0 E), having small areas from the Arctic Ocean, Norway, Sweden, Poland, Slovakia, Hungary, Serbia, Croatia, Bosnia and Herzegovina, Montenegro, Libya, Chad, Central African Republic, Democratic Republic of the Congo, Angola, Namibia, South Africa, Atlantic Ocean, Southern Ocean, and Antarctica.

Italy: 3 Nov 2009, Cividale del Friuli (founded by Julius Caesar (100 BC – 44 BC) in 50 BC with the name of Forum Iulii, 15 km east of Udine, 135 m, in the foothills of the eastern Alps, population 12,000), Piazza Foro Giulio Cesare, with nice trees.

Sub-Region R13-20E: Budapest, Rundu, Monaco

SUN: The stunning R13 comes now.

EARTH: The sub-region R13 will have the capitals in Budapest (Hungary), Rundu (Namibia), and Monaco (Monaco).
This sub-region R13 is around the meridian (longitude) 20.25^0 E $(19.5^0$ E – 21^0 E), having small areas from the Arctic Ocean, Norway, Sweden, Russia, Poland, Slovakia, Hungary, Serbia, Montenegro, Albania, Greece, Libya, Chad, Central African Republic, Democratic Republic of the Congo, Angola, Namibia, Botswana, South Africa, Atlantic Ocean, Southern Ocean, and Antarctica.

USA, Washington, DC (1790): the entrance to the Smithsonian Institution Building (1849-1855), on Jefferson Drive SW.

Sub-Region R14-22E: Belgrade, Kananga, Liverpool

SUN: Let's see the pretty R14.

EARTH: The sub-region R14 will have the capitals in Belgrade (Serbia), Kananga (Democratic Republic of Congo), and Liverpool (UK).

This sub-region R14 is around the meridian (longitude) 21.75^0 E (21^0 E – 22.5^0 E), having small areas from the Arctic Ocean, Norway, Finland, Sweden, Estonia, Latvia, Lithuania, Russia, Poland, Slovakia, Hungary, Romania, Serbia, North Macedonia, Greece, Libya, Chad, Sudan, Central African Republic, Democratic Republic of the Congo, Angola, Zambia, Namibia, Botswana, South Africa, Indian Ocean, Southern Ocean, and Antarctica.

UK, Cambridge: From the King's Parade, looking southwest to the east façade of the entrance of King's College (1441, by King Henry VI (1421-1471)).

Sub-Region R15-23E: Athens, Mongu, Los Angeles

SUN: Ready for the classical R15.

EARTH: The sub-region R15 will have the capitals in Athens (Greece), Mongu (Zambia), and Los Angeles (CA, USA). This sub-region R15 is around the meridian (longitude) 23.25^0 E, $(22.5^0$ E – 24^0 E), having small areas from the Arctic Ocean, Norway, Finland, Sweden, Estonia, Latvia, Lithuania, Poland, Ukraine, Romania, Bulgaria, Serbia, North Macedonia, Greece, Libya, Chad, Sudan, Central African Republic, Democratic Republic of the Congo, Angola, Zambia, Namibia, Botswana, South Africa, Indian Ocean, Southern Ocean, and Antarctica.

USA, Boston, 3 Dec 2009, the northeast façade of the Harvard Medical School Anno Domini 1904, founded in 1782, the graduate medical school of Harvard University, 1660 students, acceptance rate 3.7%.

Sub-Region R16-25E: Helsinki, Gaborone, Montreal

SUN: Let's see the attractive R16.

EARTH: The sub-region R16 will have the capitals in Helsinki (Finland), Gaborone (Botswana), and Montreal (Canada). This sub-region R16 is around the meridian (longitude) 24.75^0 E (24^0 E $-$ 25.5^0 E), having small areas from the Arctic Ocean, Norway, Finland, Estonia, Latvia, Lithuania, Belarus, Ukraine, Romania, Bulgaria, Greece, Libya, Egypt, Sudan, South Sudan, Central African Republic, Democratic Republic of the Congo, Zambia, Namibia, Botswana, South Africa, Indian Ocean, Southern Ocean, and Antarctica.

Finland, Helsinki: 9 May 2013, a beautiful classical building on Mikonkatu, close to Aleksanterinkatu, 200 m south-east of the Helsinki Central Railway Station, near Aleksis store.

Sub-Region R17-26E: Bucharest, Gaborone, Philadelphia

SUN: The interesting R17 is next.

EARTH: The sub-region R17 will have the capitals in Bucharest (Romania), Gaborone (Botswana), and Philadelphia (PA, USA).

This sub-region R17 is around the meridian (longitude) 26.25^0 E $(25.5^0$ E $- 27^0$ E), having small areas from the Arctic Ocean, Norway, Finland, Estonia, Latvia, Lithuania, Belarus, Ukraine, Romania, Bulgaria, Greece, Turkey, Egypt, Sudan, South Sudan, Central African Republic, Democratic Republic of the Congo, Zambia, Zimbabwe, Botswana, South Africa, Indian Ocean, Southern Ocean, and Antarctica.

USA, Newport (1639), Vinland Estate (1882, C. L. Wolfe (1828-1887), with a large Roman dolium (200 BC) near the main entrance, donated in 1955 to Salve Regina University (1934) and renamed McAuley Hall.

Sub-Region R18-28E: Minsk, Maseru, Orleans

SUN: And now the amazing R18.

EARTH: The sub-region R18 will have the capitals in Minsk (Belarus), Maseru (Lesotho), and Orleans (France).
This sub-region R18 is around the meridian (longitude) 27.75^0 E (27^0 E – 28.5^0 E), having small areas from the Arctic Ocean, Norway, Finland, Russia, Estonia, Latvia, Belarus, Ukraine, Moldova, Romania, Bulgaria, Turkey, Greece, Egypt, Sudan, South Sudan, Democratic Republic of the Congo, Zambia, Zimbabwe, Botswana, South Africa, Lesotho, Indian Ocean, Southern Ocean, and Antarctica.

France, Paris: Place de la Concorde (1772): The Egyptian obelisk (Ramses the Great, 1250 BC, 23 m), Marine Nationale (Navy, 1758, left).

Sub-Region R19-29E: Chisinau, Bujumbura, Hamburg

SUN: Finally, the remarkable R19.

EARTH: The sub-region R19 will have the capitals in Chisinau (Republic of Moldova), Bujumbura (Burundi), and Hamburg (Germany).
This sub-region R19 is around the meridian (longitude) 29.25^0 E $(28.5^0$ E $-$ 30^0 E), having small areas from the Arctic Ocean, Norway, Finland, Russia, Belarus, Ukraine, Moldova, Romania, Turkey, Egypt, Sudan, South Sudan, Democratic Republic of the Congo, Rwanda, Burundi, Zambia, Zimbabwe, Botswana, South Africa, Lesotho, Indian Ocean, Southern Ocean, and Antarctica.

Finland, Helsinki: 9 May 2013, Anttila Citycenter, commercial building south of Helsinki Central Railway Station (1907 – 1914).

3 - Region R2:30E-45E: Moscow, Cairo, Grenoble

SUN: Let's see now the third important region R2.

EARTH: Yes, R2 is defined between meridians 30^0 E and 45^0 E, with the first capitals in Moscow (Russia), Cairo (Egypt), and Grenoble (France).

SUN: This third region R2 has parts of eastern Europe, western Asia, and eastern Africa. We know the meridian 30^0 E, let's see know the meridian 45^0 E.

EARTH: The meridian 45^0 E is from the North Pole across the Arctic Ocean, Europe, Asia, Africa, the Indian Ocean, the Southern Ocean, and Antarctica to the South Pole. It passes through Russia (Island of Alexandra Land, Kanin Peninsula, Penza), Georgia, Armenia, Azerbaijan, Iran, Iraq, Saudi Arabia, Yemen. Indian Ocean, Somalia, Ethiopia, Indian Ocean, and Madagascar.

France, Grenoble (43 BC, in 381 named Gratianopolis after the 67th Emperor of the Roman Empire Gratian (359-383 (died at 24 in Lyon)), then Graignovol, population 160,000), Cours Jean Jaurès (1859-1914).

Sub-Region R20-31E: Kiev, Kigali, Ottawa

SUN: Very nice, let's start now with the first if its beautiful 10 sub-regions, R20.

EARTH: Yes, the sub-region R20 will have the capitals in Kiev (Ukraine), Kigali (Rwanda), and Ottawa (Canada).
This sub-region R20 is around the meridian (longitude) 30.75^0 E (30^0 E – 31.5^0 E), having small areas from the Arctic Ocean, Norway, Russia, Finland, Belarus, Ukraine, Turkey, Egypt, Sudan, South Sudan, Uganda, Democratic Republic of the Congo, Tanzania, Zambia, Mozambique, Zimbabwe, South Africa, Eswatini, Indian Ocean, Southern Ocean, and Antarctica.

Rome, Vatican, Piazza San Pietro (1667, by Gian Lorenzo Bernini): Basilica di San Pietro (1506, center back), granite fountain by Carlo Maderno (1614, center, north side of piazza).

Sub-Region R21-32E: Ankara, Khartoum, Salzburg

SUN: Now the dynamic R21.

EARTH: Yes, the sub-region R21 will have the capitals in Ankara (Turkey), Khartoum (Sudan), and Salzburg (Austria). This sub-region R21 is around the meridian (longitude) 32.25^0 E (31.5^0 E – 33^0 E), having small areas from the Arctic Ocean, Norway, Russia, Belarus, Ukraine, Turkey, Egypt, Sudan, South Sudan, Uganda, Tanzania, Zambia, Mozambique, Zimbabwe, South Africa, Eswatini, Indian Ocean, Southern Ocean, and Antarctica.

Finland, Helsinki: the Railway Square, east of the railway station, with the Finnish National Theatre (1872 - 1902, left).

Sub-Region R22-34E: Lilongwe, Nicosia, Dallas

SUN: Let's see the energetic R22.

EARTH: Yes, the sub-region R22 will have the capitals in Lilongwe (Malawi), Nicosia (Cyprus), and Dallas (TX, USA).
This sub-region R22 is around the meridian (longitude) 33.75^0 E (33^0 E – 34.5^0 E), having small areas from the Arctic Ocean, Russia, Ukraine, Turkey, Cyprus, Egypt, Sudan, South Sudan, Ethiopia, Kenya, Uganda, Tanzania, Malawi, Mozambique, Indian Ocean, Southern Ocean, and Antarctica.

France, Newport (1639): The west site of the Elms, 1899 - 1901, Edward Julius Berwind (1848 – 1936, coal), from Château d'Asnières (1753) in Asnières-sur-Seine (1158, 7.9 km northwest of the center of Paris, France).

Sub-Region R23-35E: Jerusalem, Dodoma, Strasbourg

SUN: Now the growing R23.

EARTH: Yes, the sub-region R23 will have the capitals in Jerusalem (Israel), Dodoma (Tanzania), and Strasbourg (France). This sub-region R23 is around the meridian (longitude) 35.25^0 E $(34.5^0$ E $- 36^0$ E), having small areas from the Arctic Ocean, Russia, Ukraine, Turkey, Israel, Jordan, Saudi Arabia, Egypt, Sudan, South Sudan, Ethiopia, Kenya, Uganda, Tanzania, Malawi, Mozambique, Indian Ocean, Southern Ocean, and Antarctica.

France, Paris: The south-west end of le Musée du Louvre (1793) near Porte Jaujard (Director of les Musées Nationaux during War World II).

Sub-Region R24-37E: Damascus, Nairobi, Stuttgart

SUN: The surprising R24 is next.

EARTH: Yes, the sub-region R24 will have the capitals in Damascus (Syria), Nairobi (Kenya), and Stuttgart (Germany).
This sub-region R24 is around the meridian (longitude) 36.75^0 E $(36^0$ E $- 37.5^0$ E), having small areas from the Arctic Ocean, Russia, Ukraine, Turkey, Syria, Jordan, Saudi Arabia, Sudan, Eritrea, Ethiopia, Kenya, Tanzania, Mozambique, Indian Ocean, Southern Ocean, and Antarctica.

Washington, D.C. (1790): a vending cart near the east side of the Smithsonian Institution Building (1849-1855), on Jefferson Drive SW, close to 7th Street SW.

Sub-Region R25-38E: Gubkin, Addis Ababa, Marseille

SUN: Now the astonishing R25.

EARTH: Yes, the sub-region R25 will have the capitals in Krasnodar (Russia), Addis Ababa (Ethiopia), and Marseille (France).

This sub-region R25 is around the meridian (longitude) 38.25^0 E $(37.5^0$ E – 39^0 E), having small areas from the Arctic Ocean, Russia, Ukraine, Turkey, Syria, Jordan, Saudi Arabia, Sudan, Eritrea, Ethiopia, Kenya, Tanzania, Mozambique, Indian Ocean, Southern Ocean, and Antarctica.

France, Paris: La Seine River, from Pont d'Arcole, near l'Hôtel de Ville (1533), with Pont Notre Dame (center-right) and Conciergerie (center).

Sub-Region R26-40E: Rostov-on-Don, Asmara, Leipzig

SUN: The astounding R26 is waiting.

EARTH: Yes, the sub-region R26 will have the capitals in Rostov-on-Don (Russia), Asmara (Eritrea), and Leipzig (Germany). This sub-region R26 is around the meridian (longitude) 39.75^0 E (39^0 E – 40.5^0 E), having small areas from the Arctic Ocean, Russia, Ukraine, Turkey, Syria, Iraq, Saudi Arabia, Eritrea, Ethiopia, Kenya, Tanzania, Mozambique, Indian Ocean, Southern Ocean, and Antarctica.

Washington, D.C. (1790): a Lunar module in The National Air and Space Museum (1976) of the Smithsonian Institution.

Sub-Region R27-41E: Stavropol, Djibuti, Zürich

SUN: Now the breathtaking R27.

EARTH: Yes, the sub-region R27 will have the capitals in Stavropol (Russia), Djibuti (Djibouti), and Zürich (Switzerland). This sub-region R27 is around the meridian (longitude) 41.25^0 E (40.5^0 E – 42^0 E), having small areas from the Arctic Ocean, Russia, Georgia, Turkey, Syria, Iraq, Saudi Arabia, Eritrea, Ethiopia, Djibouti, Somalia, Indian Ocean, Southern Ocean, and Antarctica.

Switzerland, Bern, Ristorante Azzurro Terra e Mare (left), signs for Länggasse, Universität Bern (1834), Stadtbach West and Banhnhof parking.

Sub-Region R28-43E: Mosul, Moroni, Linz

SUN: The incredible R28 is next.

EARTH: Yes, the sub-region R28 will have the capitals in Mosul (Iraq), Moroni (Comoros), and Linz (Austria)
This sub-region R28 is around the meridian (longitude) 42.75^0 E $(42^0$ E $- 43.5^0$ E), having small areas from the Arctic Ocean, Russia, Georgia, Turkey, Iraq, Saudi Arabia, Yemen, Eritrea, Ethiopia, Djibouti, Somalia, Indian Ocean, Southern Ocean, and Antarctica.

Japan, Kawaguchi, 17 km north-est of Mount Fuji (3776 m); the Kawaguchiko Railroad Station and Mount Fuji.

Sub-Region R29-44E: Yerevan, Baghdad, Göttingen

SUN: Finally, the unpredicted R29.

EARTH: Yes, the sub-region R29 will have the capitals in Yerevan (Armenia), Baghdad (Iraq), and Göttingen (Germany). This sub-region R29 is around the meridian (longitude) 44.25^0 E (43.5^0 E – 45^0 E), having small areas from the Arctic Ocean, Russia, Georgia, Armenia, Turkey, Iraq, Saudi Arabia, Yemen, Somalia, Ethiopia, Madagascar, Indian Ocean, Southern Ocean, and Antarctica.

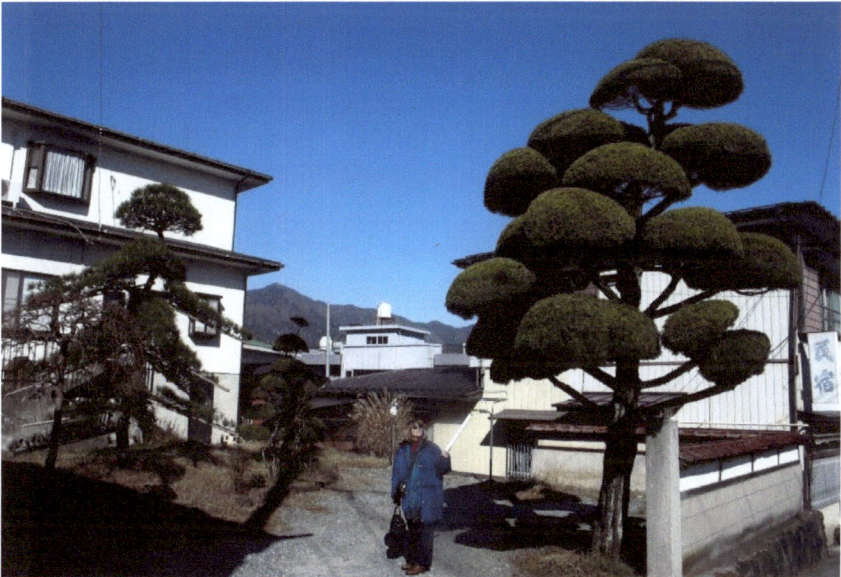

Japan, Kawaguchi, 17 km north-est of Mount Fuji (3776 m); a big Bonsai tree on the right and three smaller ones on the left.

4 - Region R3: 45E-75E Astana, Karachi, Montpellier

SUN: Let's see now the fourth magnificent region R3.

EARTH: Yes, R3 is defined between meridians 45^0 E and 75^0 E, with capitals in Astana (Kazakhstan), Karachi (Pakistan), and Montpellier (France).

SUN: The fourth region R3 has the remaining eastern Europe, and eastern Africa, and a good portion of western Asia. We know the meridian 45^0 E, let's see know the meridian 75^0 E

EARTH: The meridian 75^0 E is from the North Pole across the Arctic Ocean, Asia, the Indian Ocean, the Southern Ocean, and Antarctica. It passes through Russia, Kazakhstan, Kyrgyzstan, China, Tajikistan, Pakistan, and India.

France, Paris: Place de la Concorde (1772): the north fountain (1840, with figures of the rivers Rhone and Rhine), Hotel de Crillon (1758, left), Rue Royale, Église de la Madeleine and Marine Nationale (center).

Sub-Region R30-46E: Riyadh, Mogadishu, Bonn

SUN: Very nice, let's start now with the first if its lovely 10 sub-regions, R30.

EARTH: Yes, the sub-region R30 will have the capitals in Riyadh (Saudi Arabia), Mogadishu (Somalia), and Bonn (Germany).
This sub-region R30 is around the meridian (longitude) 46.5^0 E (45^0 E $-$ 48^0 E), having small areas from the Arctic Ocean, Russia, Georgia, Azerbaijan, Armenia, Iran, Iraq, Saudi Arabia, Yemen, Somalia, Ethiopia, Madagascar, Indian Ocean, Southern Ocean, and Antarctica.

Germany, 22 March 1978, Dortmund, the store Besta Hungshans (left), Avis rental service (center).

Sub-Region R31-49E: Baku, Antananarivo, Le Mans

SUN: Now the brilliant R31.

EARTH: Yes, the sub-region R31 will have the capitals in Baku (Azerbaijan), Antananarivo (Madagascar), and Le Mans (France).

This sub-region R31 is around the meridian (longitude) 49.5^0 E (48^0 E – 51^0 E), having small areas from the Arctic Ocean, Russia, Kazakhstan, Azerbaijan, Armenia, Iran, Saudi Arabia, Yemen, Somalia, Madagascar, Indian Ocean, Southern Ocean, and Antarctica.

France, Paris: A new entrance on the south-east part of the Gare du Nord (1846), from Place Napoléon III (1808 – 1873, nephew of Napoleon I).

Sub-Region R32-52E: Oral, Tehran, Pisa

SUN: Let's see wondrous R32.

EARTH: Yes, the sub-region R32 will have the capitals in Oral (Kazakhstan), Tehran (Iran), and Pisa (Italy).
This sub-region R32 is around the meridian (longitude) 52.5^0 E (51^0 E – 54^0 E), having small areas from the Arctic Ocean, Russia, Kazakhstan, Iran, Qatar, Saudi Arabia, Yemen, Somalia, Seychelles, Indian Ocean, Southern Ocean, and Antarctica.

Italy, 6 April 1978, Pisa, Cattedrale di Pisa (1092, striped-marble, left), Torre di Pisa (August 1173-1372, 55.86 m on the low side, 56.67 m on the high side, white-marble, 296 steps, right).

Sub-Region R33-55E: Ashgabat, Abu Dhabi, Wolfsburg

SUN: Now the delightful R33.

EARTH: Yes, the sub-region R33 will have the capitals in Ashgabat (Turkmenistan), Abu Dhabi (United Arab Emirates), and Wolfsburg (Germany).

This sub-region R33 is around the meridian (longitude) 55.5^0 E (54^0 E – 57^0 E), having small areas from the Arctic Ocean, Russia, Kazakhstan, Turkmenistan, Iran, United Arab Emirates, Saudi Arabia, Oman, Indian Ocean, Southern Ocean, and Antarctica.

Germany - 23 March 1978, Freibourg im Breisgau (1120 by Duke Berthold III of Zähringen (1085-1122), elevation 278 m, the south façade of Freiburger Münster (cathedral, 1200, 116 m, J. S. Bach (1685-1750) performed here).

Sub-Region R34-58E: Magnitogorsk, Muscat, Toulouse

SUN: The great R34 is next.

EARTH: Yes, the sub-region R34 will have the capitals in Magnitogorsk (Russia), Muscat (Oman), and Toulouse (France). This sub-region R34 is around the meridian (longitude) 58.5^0 E (57^0 E – 60^0 E), having small areas from the Arctic Ocean, Russia, Kazakhstan, Uzbekistan, Turkmenistan, Iran, Oman, Indian Ocean, Southern Ocean, and Antarctica.

France, Paris: Pavillions Richelieu (left) and Sully (right) on the north and east parts of Musée du Louvre, after Place du Carrousel and Pyramid.

Sub-Region R35-61E: Chelyabinsk, Herat, Basel

SUN: Now the terrific R35.

EARTH: Yes, the sub-region R35 will have the capitals in Chelyabinsk (Russia), Herat (Afghanistan), and Basel (Switzerland).

This sub-region R35 is around the meridian (longitude) 61.5^0 E (60^0 E – 63^0 E), having small areas from the Arctic Ocean, Russia, Kazakhstan, Uzbekistan, Turkmenistan, Iran, Afghanistan, Pakistan, Indian Ocean, Southern Ocean, and Antarctica.

Switzerland, Geneva (121 BC by Romans, 375 m elevation, population 200,000, area 16 km^2), government buildings on Quai du Mont Blanc.

Sub-Region R36-64E: Tyumen, Kandahar, Nagoya

SUN: Waiting for the awesome R36.

EARTH: Yes, the sub-region R36 will have the capitals in Tyumen (Russia), Kandahar (Afghanistan), and Nagoya (Japan). This sub-region R36 is around the meridian (longitude) 64.5^0 E (63^0 E – 66^0 E), having small areas from the Arctic Ocean, Russia, Kazakhstan, Uzbekistan, Turkmenistan, Afghanistan, Iran, Pakistan, Indian Ocean, Southern Ocean, and Antarctica.

Japan: the north side of Mount Fuji (3,776 m, 1707 last eruption) seen from Kawaguchiko (Lake Kawaguchi, 6 km^2, 830 m elevation, 100 km south-west of Tokyo, 17 km north of Mount Fuji), with a branch of a blossomed cherry.

Sub-Region R37-67E: Dushanbe, Labytnangi, Limoges

SUN: Now the grand R37.

EARTH: Yes, the sub-region R37 will have the capitals in Dushanbe (Tajikistan), Labytnangi (Russia), Limoges (France). This sub-region R37 is around the meridian (longitude) 67.5^0 E (66^0 E – 69^0 E), having small areas from the Arctic Ocean, Russia, Kazakhstan, Uzbekistan, Afghanistan, Pakistan, Indian Ocean, Southern Ocean, and Antarctica.

France, Paris: Gare Saint Lazare (1837, 27 platforms for trains towards Normandy, 100 million passengers/ year, 2nd after Gare du Nord),

Sub-Region R38-70E: Astana, Kabul, Rostock

SUN: The imposing R38 is next.

EARTH: Yes, the sub-region R38 will have the capitals in Astana (Kazakhstan), Kabul (Afghanistan), and Rostock (Germany).

This sub-region R38 is around the meridian (longitude) 70.5^0 E (69^0 E – 72^0 E), having small areas from the Arctic Ocean, Russia, Kazakhstan, Uzbekistan, Tajikistan, Afghanistan, Pakistan, India, Indian Ocean, Southern Ocean, and Antarctica.

Germany, 23 March 1978, looking west to Neuenburg am Rhein (440 km southwest of Göttingen), near the border with France, Mulheim ahead (west), Breisach left (north), Schliengen right (south).

Sub-Region R39-73E: Islamabad, Malé, La Rochelle

SUN: Finally, the impressive R39.

EARTH: Yes, the sub-region R39 will have the capitals in Islamabad (Pakistan), Malé (Maldives), and La Rochelle (France). This sub-region R39 is around the meridian (longitude) 73.5^0 E (72^0 E – 75^0 E), having small areas from the Arctic Ocean, Russia, Kazakhstan, Kyrgyzstan, Uzbekistan, Tajikistan, Afghanistan, Pakistan, India, Maldives, Indian Ocean, Southern Ocean, and Antarctica.

France, Paris: The main entrance of the old bldg. of Gare du Nord (1846, 1865).

5 - Region R4: 75E-85E: New Delhi, Novosibirsk, Magdeburg

SUN: Let's see now the fifth inspiring region R4.

EARTH: Yes, R4 is defined between meridians 75^0 E and 85^0 E, with capitals in New Delhi (India), Novosibirsk (Russia), and Magdeburg (Germany).

SUN: The fifth region R4 includes a small but densely populated area of western Asia. We know the meridian 75^0 E, let's see know the meridian 85^0 E

EARTH: The meridian 85^0 E is from the North Pole across the Arctic Ocean, Asia, the Indian Ocean, the Southern Ocean, and Antarctica. It passes through Russia, Kazakhstan, China, Nepal, and India.

Germany, 20 March 1978, Dortmund, Dortmunder Union Bier (left), Scheda (left), on a busy street only for pedestrians.

Sub-Region R40-75E: Bishkek, Jaipur, Osaka

SUN: Very nice, let's start now with the first if its 10 admirable sub-regions, R40.

EARTH: Yes, the sub-region R40 will have the capitals in Bishkek (Kyrgyzstan), Jaipur (India), and Osaka (Japan).
This sub-region R40 is around the meridian (longitude) 75.5^0 E (75^0 E $- 76^0$ E), having small areas from the Arctic Ocean, Russia, Kazakhstan, Kyrgyzstan, China, Tajikistan, Pakistan, India, Indian Ocean, Southern Ocean, and Antarctica.

Japan, Osaka, very nice flower arrangement coming from a basket, near the north side of the Osaka Castle (1597).

Sub-Region R41-76E: Akola, Kashgar, and Genoa

SUN: Now the fine R41.

EARTH: Yes, the sub-region R41 will have the capitals in Akola (India), Kashgar (China), and Genoa (Italy).
This sub-region R41 is around the meridian (longitude) 76.5^0 E (76^0 E – 77^0 E), having small areas from the Arctic Ocean, Russia, Kazakhstan, Kyrgyzstan, China, Pakistan, India, Indian Ocean, Southern Ocean, and Antarctica.

Italy: 3 Nov 2009, Palazzo Comunale (1350-1550) di Cividale

Sub-Region R42-77E: Almaty, Coimbatore, Perth

SUN: Let's see the acclaimed R42.

EARTH: Yes, the sub-region R42 will have the capitals in Almaty (Kazakhstan), Coimbatore (India), and Perth (Australia). This sub-region R42 is around meridian (longitude) 77.5^0 E (77^0 E – 78^0 E), having small areas from the Arctic Ocean, Kara Sea, Russia, Kazakhstan, Kyrgyzstan, China, Pakistan, India, Indian Ocean, Southern Ocean and Antarctica.

Australia: Looking northwest to the southeast side of the northern part of Sydney Harbour Bridge (1932, 134 m height (the tallest in the world), length 1,149 m, width 49 m, 49 m above water).

Sub-Region R43-78E: Kuybyshev, Agra, Fukuoka

SUN: Now the renowned R43.

EARTH: Yes, the sub-region R43 will have the capitals in Kuybyshev (Russia), Agra (India), and Fukuoka (Japan).
This sub-region R43 is around meridian (longitude) 78.5^0 E (78^0 E – 79^0 E), having small areas from the Arctic Ocean, Kara Sea, Russia, Kazakhstan, Kyrgyzstan, China, India, Indian Ocean, Southern Ocean and Antarctica.

Japan, Tokyo, the East Gardens of the Imperial Palace: the remains of the main tower Tenshudai (left walls, 1607, destroyed 1657).

Sub-Region R44-79E: Vertikos, Nagpur, Coral Bay

SUN: Next is the proud R44.

EARTH: Yes, the sub-region R44 will have the capitals in Vertikos (Russia), Nagpur (India), and Coral Bay (Australia).
This sub-region R44 is around meridian (longitude) 79.5^0 E (79^0 E – 80^0 E), having small areas from the Arctic Ocean, Kara Sea, Russia, Kazakhstan, Kyrgyzstan, China, India, Indian Ocean, Southern Ocean and Antarctica.

Australia: The ship Fairstar in the Sydney Harbour, near the Opera House.

Sub-Region R45-80E: Chennai, Colombo, Sapporo

SUN: Now the notable R45.

EARTH: Yes, the sub-region R45 will have the capitals in Chennai (India), Colombo (Sri Lanka), and Sapporo (Japan).
This sub-region R45 is around meridian (longitude) 80.5^0 E (80^0 E – 81^0 E), having small areas from the Arctic Ocean, Kara Sea, Russia, Kazakhstan, Kyrgyzstan, China, India, Sri Lanka, Indian Ocean, Southern Ocean and Antarctica.

Japan, Tokyo: on a street 75 m east of Kanda Myojin Shrine (744), a Shinto shrine located in Chiyoda (Nihonbashi).

Sub-Region R46-81E: Lucknow, Fedosikha, Niigata

SUN: The good R46 is waiting.

EARTH: Yes, the sub-region R46 will have the capitals in Lucknow (India), Fedosikha (Russia), and Niigata (Japan).
This sub-region R46 is around meridian (longitude) 81.5^0 E (81^0 E – 82^0 E), having small areas from the Arctic Ocean, Kara Sea, Russia, Kazakhstan, China, Nepal, India, Sri Lanka, Indian Ocean, Southern Ocean and Antarctica.

Japan: the north side of Mount Fuji (3,776 m) seen from Kawaguchi city, near Kawaguchiko (Lake Kawaguchi, down right), 100 km south-west of Tokyo, 17 km north of Mount Fuji.

Sub-Region R47-82E: Bilaspur, Kolpashevo, Albany

SUN: Now the accomplished R47.

EARTH: Yes, the sub-region R47 will have the capitals in Bilaspur (India), Kolpashevo (Russia), and Albany (Australia).
This sub-region R47 is around meridian (longitude) 82.5^0 E (82^0 E – 83^0 E), having small areas from the Arctic Ocean, Kara Sea, Russia, Kazakhstan, China, Nepal, India, Indian Ocean, Southern Ocean, and Antarctica.

Looking northeast to the southwest side of the harbourfront Sydney Opera House (1959-1973).

Sub-Region R48-83E: Visakhapatnam, Barnaul, Hiroshima

SUN: Ready for the capable R48.

EARTH: Yes, the sub-region R48 will have the capitals in Visakhapatnam (India), Barnaul (Russia), and Hiroshima (Japan). This sub-region R48 is around meridian (longitude) 83.5^0 E (83^0 E – 84^0 E), having small areas from the Arctic Ocean, Kara Sea, Russia, Kazakhstan, China, Nepal, India, Indian Ocean, Southern Ocean, and Antarctica.

Japan, Hiroshima, 17 April 2015, Bell of Peace (1964), The Greek inscription on the bell is Socrates' (469 BC – 399 BC) aphorism "Know yourself".

Sub-Region R49-84E: Brahmapur, Tomsk, Yokohama

SUN: Finally, the gifted R49.

EARTH: Yes, the sub-region R49 will have the capitals in Brahmapur (India), Tomsk (Russia), and Yokohama (Japan).
This sub-region R49 is around meridian (longitude) 84.5^0 E (84^0 E – 85^0 E), having small areas from the Arctic Ocean, Kara Sea, Russia, Kazakhstan, China, Nepal, India, Indian Ocean, Southern Ocean, and Antarctica.

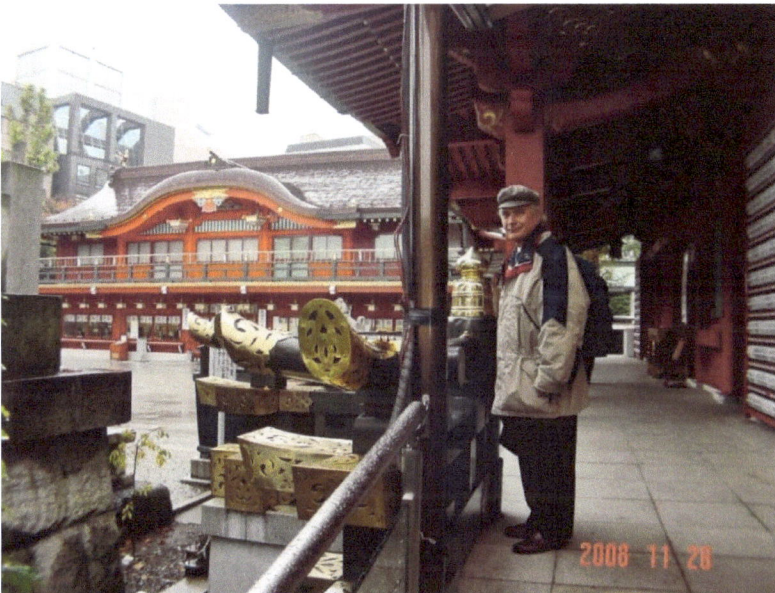

Japan, Tokyo: Edo Sochiaju Kanda Myojin, Kanda Shrine (right), the Tutelary Shrine of All Edo (744), a Shinto shrine located in Chiyoda (Nihonbashi), 2 km north-east of the Imperial Palace.

6 - Region R5: 85E–100E: Krasnoyarsk, Urumqi, Avignon

SUN: Let's see now the 6th talented region R5.

EARTH: Yes, R5 is defined between meridians 85^0 E and 100^0 E, with capitals in Krasnoyarsk (Russia), Urumqi (China), and Avignon (France).

SUN: The 6th region R5 contains a part of the central-west Asia. We know the meridian 85^0 E, let's see know the meridian 100^0 E

EARTH: The meridian 100^0 E is from the North Pole across the Arctic Ocean, Asia, the Indian Ocean, the Southern Ocean, and Antarctica. It passes through Russia, Mongolia, China, Myanmar, Thailand, and Indonesia.

USA, Boston, 20 June 2015, Boston Public Garden (1837, 9.7 ha, 1 km south of MGH, adjacent to Boston Common), Swan Boats.

France, Paris: A copy (made in 1964) of the sculpture "The Dance" (1868 – 1869, 4.2 m by 3 m, with a highly animated central male dancer, surrounded by six dancing women (the original is now in the Musée d'Orsay)) by Jean-Baptiste Carpeaux (1827 – 1875, he closely studied the sculpture of Michelangelo (1475 – 1564) in Rome; Garnier commissioned Carpeaux in 1865), on the left side of the right outer bay on the façade of l'Opéra de Paris (1875).

Sub-Region R50-86E: Kathmandu, Patna, Kobe

SUN: Good, let's start now with the first if its 10 seasoned sub-regions, R50.

EARTH: Yes, the sub-region R50 will have the capitals in Kathmandu (Nepal), Patna (India), and Kobe (Japan).

This sub-region R50 is around the meridian (longitude) 85.75^0 E (85^0 E – 86.5^0 E), having small areas from the Arctic Ocean, Kara Sea, Russia, Kazakhstan, China, Nepal, India, Indian Ocean, Southern Ocean, and Antarctica.

Japan, Kobe: 24 Nov 2008, Kobe (201 AD, the 5th largest city in Japan, 30 km west of Osaka), Shin-Kobe Oriental Hotel C3 building (center back, 158 m, 37 floors, 1988).

Sub-Region R51-87E: Bayingol, Novokuznetsk, Vichy

SUN: Now the able R51.

EARTH: Yes, the sub-region R51 will have the capitals in Bayingol (China), Novokuznetsk (Russia), and Vichy (France).
This sub-region R51 is around the meridian (longitude) 87.25^0 E (86.5^0 E – 88^0 E), having small areas from the Arctic Ocean, Kara Sea, Russia, Kazakhstan, China, Nepal, India, Indian Ocean, Southern Ocean, and Antarctica.

L'Opéra de Paris (or L'Académie Nationale de Musique, or l'Opéra Garnier, or Le Palais Garnier, or L'Opéra), a 1,979-seat opera house, built from 1861 to 1875, now mainly used for ballet.

Sub-Region R52-89E: Thimphu, Dhaka, Jena

SUN: Next will be the proficient R52.

EARTH: Yes, the sub-region R52 will have the capitals in Thimphu (Bhutan), Dhaka (Bangladesh), and Jena (Germany).
This sub-region R52 is around the meridian (longitude) 88.75^0 E (88^0 E – 89.5^0 E), having small areas from the Arctic Ocean, Kara Sea, Russia, Mongolia, China, Bhutan, India, Bangladesh, Indian Ocean, Southern Ocean, and Antarctica.

Germany, 20 March 1978, Dortmund, Pezzer (center), Pelze (left).

Sub-Region R53-90E: Lhasa, Achinsk, Reims

SUN: Now the qualified R53.

EARTH: Yes, the sub-region R53 will have the capitals in Lhasa (China), Achinsk (Russia), and Reims (France).
This sub-region R53 is around meridian (longitude) 90.25^0 E (89.5^0 E – 91^0 E), having small areas from the Arctic Ocean, Kara Sea, Russia, Mongolia, China, Bhutan, India, Bangladesh, Indian Ocean, Southern Ocean, and Antarctica.

France, Paris: the façade of the Centre Georges Pompidou (1971 – 1977, Beaubourg area). Georges Pompidou (1911 – 1974) was President of France (1969 – 1974) and Prime Minister (1962 – 1968).

Sub-Region R54-92E: Abakan, Kumul, Fribourg

SUN: The competent R54 is coming.

EARTH: Yes, the sub-region R54 will have the capitals in Abakan (Russia), Kumul (China), and Fribourg (Switzerland). This sub-region R54 is around meridian (longitudes) 91.75^0 E (91^0 E $- 92.5^0$ E), having small areas from the Arctic Ocean, Kara Sea, Russia, Mongolia, China, Bhutan, India, Bangladesh, Indian Ocean, Southern Ocean, and Antarctica.

Switzerland, Geneva (121 BC), from Quai du Mont Blanc, looking northeast at Rue des Alpes, northwest of the Monument Brunswick (right).

Sub-Region R55-93E: Kyzyl, Dibrugarh, Denmark

SUN: Now the efficient R55.

EARTH: Yes, the sub-region R55 will have the capitals in Kyzyl (Russia), Dibrugarh (India), and Denmark (Australia).
This sub-region R55 is around meridian (longitude) 93.25^0 E (92.5^0 E – 94^0 E), having small areas from the Arctic Ocean, Kara Sea, Russia, Mongolia, China, India, Myanmar, Indian Ocean, Southern Ocean, and Antarctica.

Australia: From the Royal Botanic Gardens looking northwest to the southeast side of the harbourfront Sydney Opera House (1959-1973).

Sub-Region R56-95E: Bassein, Tinsukia, Chiba

SUN: Waiting for the effective R56.

EARTH: Yes, the sub-region R56 will have the capitals in Bassein (Myanmar), Tinsukia (India), and Chiba (Japan).
This sub-region R56 is around the meridian (longitude) 94.75^0 E (94^0 E – 95.5^0 E), having small areas from the Arctic Ocean, Kara Sea, Russia, Mongolia, China, India, Myanmar, Indian Ocean, Southern Ocean, and Antarctica.

Japan: Chiba Newtown Chuo Station on Hokuso Line (after Inzai-makinohara, before Komuro), 35 km north-east of Tokyo Imperial Palace, 24 km east of Narita International Airport: Hokuso Line Guide.

Sub-Region R57-96E: Yushu City, Tinskoy, Klagenfurt

SUN: Now the gifted R57.

EARTH: Yes, the sub-region R57 will have the capitals in Yushu City (China), Tinskoy (Russia), and Klagenfurt (Austria). This sub-region R57 is around the meridian (longitude) 96.25^0 E (95.5^0 E – 97^0 E), having small areas from the Arctic Ocean, Kara Sea, Russia, Mongolia, China, India, Myanmar, Indian Ocean, Indonesia, Southern Ocean, and Antarctica.

France, 18 May 1978, Station de ski du Schnepfenried, 3 km southwest of Sondernach, 50 km west of Rhine, Le Chalet Amis de la Nature, elevation 1,050 m in the Vosgien Mountain.

Sub-Region R58-98E: Jiuquan, Medan, Lucerne

SUN: The expert R58 is next.

EARTH: Yes, the sub-region R58 will have the capitals in Jiuquan (China), Medan (Indonesia), and Lucerne (Switzerland). This sub-region R58 is around meridian (longitudes) 97.75^0 E (97^0 E – 98.5^0 E), having small areas from the Arctic Ocean, Laptev Sea, Russia, Mongolia, China, Myanmar, Thailand, Indian Ocean, Indonesia, Southern Ocean, and Antarctica.

Switzerland, Lausanne (Roman 150, 147,000, 41 km^2, 500 m elevation, 62 km northeast of Geneva, the home of the International Olympic Committee), marina on Lac Léman, southwest of Place de la Navigation (right).

Sub-Region R59-99E: Chiang Mai, Dehong, Mulhouse

SUN: Finally, the versed R59.

EARTH: Yes, the sub-region R59 will have the capitals in Chiang Mai (Thailand), Dehong (China), and Mulhouse (France). This sub-region R59 is around meridian (longitudes) 99.25^0 E (98.5^0 E – 100^0 E), having small areas from the Arctic Ocean, Laptev Sea, Russia, Mongolia, China, Myanmar, Thailand, Indian Ocean, Indonesia, Southern Ocean, and Antarctica.

France, Paris: Gare de l'Est (1849, 30 platforms for Strasbourg, Mulhouse, Venice Simplon Orient Express), in Place du 11 Novembre 1918.

7 - Region R6: 100E-115E: Jakarta, Beijing, Neuchâtel

SUN: Let's see now the 7th excellent region R6.

EARTH: Yes, R6 is defined between meridians 100^0 E and 115^0 E, with capitals in Jakarta (Indonesia), Beijing (China), and Neuchâtel (Switzerland).

SUN: This 7th region R6 contains part of the central Asia and of the western Australia. We know the meridian 100^0 E, let's see know the meridian 115^0 E

EARTH: The meridian 115^0 E is from the North Pole across the Arctic Ocean, Asia, the Indian Ocean, Australia, the Southern Ocean, and Antarctica to the South Pole. It passes through Russia, Mongolia, China, Brunei, Malaysia, Indonesia, and Australia.

Switzerland, Neuchâtel, on Avenue du Premier Mars, Place Numa Droz, Quai du Port (right), a classic building with La Poste and above the upper 4 windows it is written France, Russie, Allemagne, Italie.

Sub-Region R60-101E: Bangkok, Kuala Lumpur, Besançon

SUN: Good, let's start now with the first if its 10 professional sub-regions, R60.

EARTH: Yes, the sub-region R60 will have the capitals in Bangkok (Thailand), Kuala Lumpur (Malaysia), and Besançon (France).

This sub-region R60 is around meridian (longitude) 100.75^0 E (100^0 E – 101.5^0 E), having small areas from the Arctic Ocean, Laptev Sea, Russia, Mongolia, China, Myanmar, Laos, Thailand, Malaysia, Indonesia, Indian Ocean, Southern Ocean, and Antarctica.

Paris, Île de la Cité, Pont au Change (1860): La Conciergerie (Palace of French Kings (950 – 1358), on Quai de l'Horloge, left), Pont Neuf (1578-1607, center, at the west corner of Île de la Cité).

Sub-Region R61:102E: Vientiane, Singapore, Freiburg im Breisgau

SUN: Now the ingenious R61.

EARTH: Yes, the sub-region R61 will have the capitals in Vientiane (Laos), Singapore, and Freiburg im Breisgau (Germany). This sub-region R61 is around meridian (longitude) 102.25^0 E (101.5^0 E – 103^0 E), having small areas from the Arctic Ocean, Laptev Sea, Russia, Mongolia, China, Laos, Thailand, Malaysia, Indonesia, Indian Ocean, Southern Ocean, and Antarctica.

France, Paris, on a boat on la Seine, looking upstream, east: Quai du Marché Neuf (left) and the west façade of Notre Dame (1163-1345, center right) on l'Île de la Cité, Petit Pont (50 BC in Roman Lutetia Parisiorum, 1853, right).

Sub-Region R62-104E: Phnom Penh, Irkutsk, Baden

SUN: Ready for the marvelous R62.

EARTH: Yes, the sub-region R62 will have the capitals in Phnom Penh (Cambodia), Irkutsk (Russia), and Baden (Switzerland).
This sub-region R62 is around meridian (longitude) 103.75^0 E (103^0 E – 104.5^0 E), having small areas from the Arctic Ocean, Laptev Sea, Russia, Mongolia, China, Vietnam, Laos, Thailand, Cambodia, Malaysia, Singapore, Indonesia, Indian Ocean, Southern Ocean, and Antarctica.

Switzerland, Bern (1191, the capital city of Switzerland, on Aare River, 140,000, 52 km², 130 km northeast of Geneva), on Bühlstrasse, at Depotstrasse (left), 150 m south of the Institut fur Rechtsmedizin der Universität Bern (1834, 15,000 students).

Sub-Region R63-105E: Palembang, Hanoi, Thun

SUN: Now the spectacular R63.

EARTH: Yes, the sub-region R63 will have the capitals in Palembang (Indonesia), Hanoi (Vietnam), and Thun (Switzerland). This sub-region R63 is around meridian (longitude) 105.25^0 E (104.5^0 E – 106^0 E), having small areas from the Arctic Ocean, Laptev Sea, Russia, Mongolia, China, Vietnam, Laos, Thailand, Cambodia, Indonesia, Indian Ocean, Southern Ocean, and Antarctica.

Switzerland, Geneva, Broken Chair Sculpture (1997, 2007, 12 m, 5.5 tons of wood, to protest cluster bombs & land mines) in Place des Nations.

Sub-Region R64-107E: Ulan Bator, Ulan-Ude, Chaumont

SUN: The stupendous R64 is next.

EARTH: Yes, the sub-region R64 will have the capitals in Ulan Bator (Mongolia), Ulan-Ude (Russia), and Chaumont (France).
This sub-region R64 is around meridian (longitude) 106.75^0 E (106^0 E – 107.5^0 E), having small areas from the Arctic Ocean, Laptev Sea, Russia, Mongolia, China, Vietnam, South China Sea, Laos, Cambodia, Indonesia, Indian Ocean, Southern Ocean, and Antarctica.

France, Paris, La Seine: the north end of Pont Neuf (1578-1607, the oldest bridge in Paris, at the west corner of Île de la Cité), Grands Magasins de la Samaritaine (1869, center).

Sub-Region R65-108E: Cirebon, Nanning, Vaduz

SUN: Now the prodigious R65.

EARTH: Yes, the sub-region R65 will have the capitals in Cirebon (Indonesia), Nanning (China), and Vaduz (Lichtenstein). This sub-region R65 is around meridian (longitude) 108.25^0 E (107.5^0 E – 109^0 E), having small areas from the Arctic Ocean, Laptev Sea, Russia, Mongolia, China, Vietnam, South China Sea, Indonesia, Indian Ocean, Southern Ocean, and Antarctica.

France, Paris: On a boat sur la Seine, looking upstream, northeast, to the left bank (right): Port de Grenelle (right), near Quai de Grenelle, the southwest side of la Tour Eiffel (1889, 324 m), Île aux Cygnes (left), a bridge for railroad, and after it Pont de Bir-Hakeim (1905).

Sub-Region R66-110E: Pontianak, Baotou, Lugano

SUN: The next is the awesome R66.

EARTH: Yes, the sub-region R66 will have the capitals in Pontianak (Indonesia), Baotou (China), and Lugano (Switzerland). This sub-region R66 is around meridian (longitude) 109.75^0 E (109^0 E – 110.5^0 E), having small areas from the Arctic Ocean, Laptev Sea, Russia, Mongolia, China, South China Sea, Malaysia, Indonesia, Indian Ocean, Southern Ocean, and Antarctica.

Switzerland, Geneva, on Rue de Lausanne at Av. de la Paix (left), in Place Albert Thomas (1878-1932, politician), across WTO (World Trade Org),

Sub-Region R67-111E: Surakarta, Yichang, Thonon-les-Bain

SUN: Now the superb R67.

EARTH: Yes, the sub-region R67 will have the capitals in Surakarta (Indonesia), Yichang (China), and Thonon-les-Bain (France).

This sub-region R67 is around meridian (longitude) 111.25^0 E (110.5^0 E – 112^0 E), having small areas from the Arctic Ocean, Laptev Sea, Russia, Mongolia, China, South China Sea, Malaysia, Indonesia, Indian Ocean, Southern Ocean, and Antarctica.

Tour Eiffel (1889, 324 m, looking north-west): Tour Eiffel shadow (right), Pont d'Iéna over La Seine (center down), Jardin du Trocadéro (center), Chaillot Palace (middle), tall buildings in Courbevoie near La Seine (up center, 4.5 km away).

Sub-Region R68-113E: Surabaya, Changsha, Burgdorf

SUN: The picturesque R68 is waiting.

EARTH: Yes, the sub-region R68 will have the capitals in Surabaya (Indonesia), Changsha (China), and Burgdorf (Switzerland).
This sub-region R68 is around meridian (longitude) 112.75^0 E (112^0 E – 113.5^0 E), having small areas from the Arctic Ocean, Laptev Sea, Russia, Mongolia, China, South China Sea, Malaysia, Indonesia, Indian Ocean, Australia, Southern Ocean, and Antarctica.

Switzerland, Geneva, on Pont du Mont Blanc (1862, 1965, 252 m X 26.8 m, over Rhône river), going northwest, looking west to Pont des Bergues and a tree from Île Rousseau (1712-1778, left).

Sub-Region R69-114E: Chita, Hong Kong, Colmar

SUN: Finally, the scenic R69.

EARTH: Yes, the sub-region R69 will have the capitals in Chita (Russia), Hong Kong (China), and Colmar (France).
This sub-region R69 is around meridian (longitude) 114.25^0 E (113.5^0 E – 115^0 E), having small areas from the Arctic Ocean, Laptev Sea, Russia, Mongolia, China, South China Sea, Malaysia, Indonesia, Indian Ocean, Australia, Southern Ocean, and Antarctica.

Paris, Île de la Cité: the oldest public clock in France (left, built in 1370 with a mechanism from 1334), at the north-est corner of La Conciergerie, the Palace of French Kings from 950 until 1358.

8 - Region R7: 115E-180: Tokyo, Sydney, Malmö

SUN: Let's see now the 8th charming region R7.

EARTH: Yes, R7 is defined between meridians 115^0 E and 180^0, with capitals in Tokyo (Japan), Sydney (Australia), and Malmö (Sweden).

Sweden, Malmö, from Skeppsbron looking north to the north part of the west side of the Central Station (right), sign for Trelleborg and Limhamn (to left), Goteborg and Hamnen (straight).

SUN: This 8th region R7 contains part of the eastern Asia and of the remaining of Australia, with many islands in the western Pacific. We know the meridian 115^0 E, let's see know the meridian 180^0

EARTH: The 180th meridian, or antemeridian, is the meridian 180° both east and west of the Prime Meridian, with which it forms a great circle dividing the Earth into the Western and Eastern Hemispheres. It is common to both east longitude and west longitude. It mostly passes through the open waters of the Pacific Ocean, but passes across land in Russia, Fiji and Antarctica. This meridian is used as the basis for the International Date Line.

The meridian 180^0 is from the North Pole across the Arctic Ocean, Russia, the Pacific Ocean, Fiji, the Southern Ocean, and Antarctica to the South Pole.

Australia, From the sidewalk west of the Sydney Opera House, looking southwest to the center of Sydney.

Japan, Tokyo: The west side of Tokyo Skytree. The broadcasting, restaurant, and observation tower is located in Sumida, 5 km north-east of the Imperial Palace. 634 m in March 2011, making it the tallest tower in the world, and the second tallest structure in the world. Without antenna it is 495 m, top observation floor is at 451.2 m, and the second observation floor is at 350 m. It has 13 elevators. The exterior lattice is painted a color called "Skytree White". The tower is illuminated using LED lights.

Sub-Region R70: 116E: Bandar Seri Begawan, Nanchang, Turku

SUN: Good, let's start now with the first if its 10 pleasing sub-regions, R70.

EARTH: Yes, the sub-region R70 will have the capitals in Bandar Seri Begawan (Brunei Darussalam), Nanchang (China), and Turku (Finland).
This sub-region R70 is around meridian (longitude) 116^0 E (115^0 E – 117^0 E), having small areas from the Arctic Ocean, Laptev Sea, Russia, Mongolia, China, South China Sea, Malaysia, Indonesia, Indian Ocean, Australia, Southern Ocean, and Antarctica.

Finland, Helsinki: 9 May 2013, Diacor, RAX and other stores near Helsinki Central Railway Station (1907 – 1914).

Sub-Region R71-118E: Krasnokamensk, Jinan, St. Gallen

SUN: Now the engaging R71.

EARTH: Yes, the sub-region R71 will have the capitals in Krasnokamensk (Russia), Jinan (China), and St. Gallen (Switzerland).

This sub-region R71 is around meridian (longitude) 118^0 E (117^0 E – 119^0 E), having small areas from the Arctic Ocean, Laptev Sea, Russia, Mongolia, China, South China Sea, Philippines, Malaysia, Indonesia, Indian Ocean, Australia, Southern Ocean, and Antarctica.

Switzerland, Lausanne-Ouchy Ferry Terminal on Lac Léman, south of Le Château d'Ouchy (left, 1170, 1464, rebuilt 1889-1893).

Sub-Region R72-120E: Baguio City, Hangzhou, Dole

SUN: Next is the cute R72.

EARTH: Yes, the sub-region R72 will have the capitals in Baguio City (Philippines), Hangzhou (China), and Dole (France). This sub-region R72 is around meridian (longitude) 120^0 E (119^0 E – 121^0 E), having small areas from the Arctic Ocean, Laptev Sea, Russia, China, East China Sea, South China Sea, Philippines, Indonesia, Indian Ocean, Australia, Southern Ocean, and Antarctica.

France, Paris: La Seine, on Parisis boat, looking downriver: Pont du Carrousel, 1831-1834, between the Place du Carrousel (part of Musée du Louvre (1793), right) and the Quai Voltaire (left).

Sub-Region R73-122E: Manila, Taipei, Metz

SUN: Now the adorable R73.

EARTH: Yes, the sub-region R73 will have the capitals in Manila (Philippines), Taipei (Taiwan, China), and Metz (France). This sub-region R73 is around meridian (longitude) 122^0 E (121^0 E $- 123^0$ E), having small areas from the Arctic Ocean, Laptev Sea, Russia, China, Yellow Sea, East China Sea, Pacific Ocean, Philippines, Indonesia, Indian Ocean, Australia, Southern Ocean, and Antarctica.

USA, California, from Pacifica State Beach (south of San Francisco), looking west to the Pacific Ocean (165,250,000 km^2).

Sub-Region R74-124E: Kupang, Shanghai, Davos

SUN: Ready for the graceful R74.

EARTH: Yes, the sub-region R74 will have the capitals in Kupang (Indonesia), Shanghai (China), and Davos (Switzerland). This sub-region R74 is around meridian (longitude) 124^0 E (123^0 E – 125^0 E), having small areas from the Arctic Ocean, Laptev Sea, Russia, China, Yellow Sea, East China Sea, Japan, Pacific Ocean, Philippines, Indonesia, Indian Ocean, Australia, Southern Ocean, and Antarctica.

Switzerland, Neuchâtel (150, 430 m, 33,000, 100 km northeast of Geneva, 18 km^2), Banque Cantonale Neuchâteloise (1883), in Place Pury.

Sub-Region R75-126E: Pyongyang, Seoul, Versailles

SUN: Now the glamorous R75.

EARTH: Yes, the sub-region R75 will have the capitals in Pyongyang (North Korea), Seoul (South Korea), and Versailles (France).
This sub-region R75 is around meridian (longitude) 126^0 E (125^0 E – 127^0 E), having small areas from the Arctic Ocean, Laptev Sea, Russia, China, North Korea, Yellow Sea, South Korea, East China Sea, Pacific Ocean, Philippines, Indonesia, Timor-Leste, Indian Ocean, Australia, Southern Ocean, and Antarctica.

La Seine, on Parisis boat, looking to the left bank: Musée d'Orsay (1986, former Gare d'Orsay (1898-1900)), on Rue de la Légion d'Honneur, Quai Anatole France, near Port de Solférino.

Sub-Region R76-129E: Vladivostok, Busan, Innsbruck

SUN: The stylish R76 is waiting.

EARTH: Yes, the sub-region R76 will have the capitals in Vladivostok (Russia), Busan (South Korea), and Innsbruck (Austria).
This sub-region R76 is around meridian (longitude) 129^0 E (127^0 E – 131^0 E), having small areas from the Arctic Ocean, Laptev Sea, Russia, China, North Korea, Sea of Japan, South Korea, East China Sea, Japan, Pacific Ocean, Indonesia, Australia, Southern Ocean, and Antarctica.

Italy, 20 April 1978, Milano, in Piazza della Scala (Largo Antonio Ghiringhelli (1906-1979, left), looking northwest to the southeast façade of Teatro alla Scala (3 August 1778, capacity 2,800).

Sub-Region R77-134E: Kyoto, Khabarovsk, Germering

SUN: Now the refined R77.

EARTH: Yes, the sub-region R77 will have the capitals in Kyoto (Japan), Khabarovsk (Russia), and Germering (Germany). This sub-region R77 is around meridian (longitude) 133.5^0 E (131^0 E – 136^0 E), having small areas from the Arctic Ocean, Laptev Sea, Russia, Sea of Japan, Japan, Pacific Ocean, Indonesia, Australia, Southern Ocean, and Antarctica.

Japan, Kyoto, a double gate of the Higashi Honganji temple (1602, or the Eastern Temple of the Original Vow)

Sub-Region R78-139E: Nagoya, Komsomolsk-on-Amur, Venice

SUN: Let's see the sophisticated R78.

EARTH: Yes, the sub-region R78 will have the capitals in Nagoya (Japan), Komsomolsk-on-Amur (Russia), and Venice (Italy).

This sub-region R78 is around meridian (longitude) 138.5^0 E (136^0 E – 141^0 E), having small areas from the Arctic Ocean, Laptev Sea, Russia, Sea of Japan, Japan, Pacific Ocean, Indonesia, Australia, Southern Ocean, and Antarctica.

Italy, 29 Sep 2008, Venezia (421), Piazza San Marco (1084) looking north, Torre dell'Orologio (1499, left back), Basilica di San Marco (1173, center back), .Palazzo Ducale (Doge's Palace, 1424, right).

Sub-Region R79-145E: Sendai, Melbourne, St. Moritz

SUN: Finally, the exquisite R79.

EARTH: Yes, the sub-region R79 will have the capitals in Sendai (Japan), Melbourne (Australia), and St. Moritz (Switzerland).

This sub-region R79 is around meridian (longitude) 145^0 E (141^0 E $- 180^0$), having some larger areas from the Arctic Ocean, Russia, Sea of Okhotsk, Japan, Pacific Ocean, Papua New Guinea, Australia, New Zealand, Southern Ocean, and Antarctica.

Japan: Matsushima (20 km north-east of Sendai, with a beautiful bay, dotted by pine clad islets; it is the most scenic view of Japan). To the right: Matsushima Kaigan Station, 650 m, Zuiganji Zen Temple, 500 m, Godaido Temple, 100m. To the left, Fukuurajima Island, accessible via a long bridge, 650 m.

9 - Region R8: 180-70W: Washington, Mexico City, Bellinzona

SUN: Let's see now the 9th cosmopolitan region R8.

EARTH: Yes, R8 is defined between meridians 180^0 - 70^0 W, with capitals in Washington (USA), Mexico City (Mexico), and Bellinzona (Switzerland).

USA, Mount Washington Resort, Bretton Woods, New Hampshire, where the United Nations Monetary and Financial Conference took place in July 1944.

SUN: This 9th region R8 contains just a small part of the eastern Asia and of the western parts of Americas, with many islands in the eastern Pacific. We know the meridian 180^0, let's see know the meridian 70^0 W.

EARTH: The meridian 70^0 W is from the North Pole across the Arctic Ocean, North America, the Atlantic Ocean, the Caribbean Sea, South America, the Pacific Ocean, the Southern Ocean, and

Antarctica to the South Pole, passing through Canada, Greenland, United States, Dominican Republic, Aruba, Venezuela, Colombia, Brazil, Peru, Chile, Argentina.

Switzerland, on the road from Martigny to Saint-Maurice

Sub-Region R80-150W: Uelen, Anchorage, Zug

SUN: Good, let's start now with the first if its 10 proficient sub-regions, R80, which is mostly over the Pacific Ocean, and, most importantly, connects Asia with America.

EARTH: Yes, the sub-region R80 will have the capitals in Uelen (Russia), Anchorage (Alaska, USA), and Zug (Switzerland). This sub-region R80 is around meridian (longitude) 150^0 W (180^0 – 130^0 W), having same larger areas from the Arctic Ocean, little from Russia, more from USA, Canada, Pacific Ocean, Southern Ocean, and Antarctica.

Switzerland, Geneva (121 BC under Romans), Avenue de la Paix 19, International Committee of the Red Cross founded by Jean Henri Dunant (1828-1910) on Feb. 9, 1863, three Nobel Peace Prizes.

Sub-Region R81-122W: Vancouver, San Jose, Odense

SUN: Now the trained R81.

EARTH: Yes, the sub-region R81 will have the capitals in Vancouver (Canada), San Jose (CA, USA), and Odense (Denmark). This sub-region R81 is around meridian (longitude) 122^0 W (130^0 W – 121^0 W), having small areas from the Arctic Ocean, Canada, USA, Pacific Ocean, Southern Ocean, and Antarctica.

USA, California, Berkeley, Claremont Club & Spa, A Fairmont Hotel, 2 km southeast of the University of California, Berkeley.

Sub-Region R82-119W: Vernon, Los Angeles, Amstetten

SUN: Let's see the virtuoso R82.

EARTH: Yes, the sub-region R82 will have the capitals in Vernon (Canada), Los Angeles (CA, USA), and Amstetten (Austria).

This sub-region R82 is around meridian (longitude) 119^0 W (121^0 W – 117^0 W), having small areas from the Arctic Ocean, Canada, USA, Pacific Ocean, Southern Ocean, and Antarctica.

USA, UC Berkeley (1868), 21 December 2014, from Campanile (1914, 94 m) looking north: Mathematics Dep. (Evans Hall, center), Hearst Memorial Mining Bldg (next right), Hearst Mining Circle (green center right), Earth Sciences and Map Library (left).

Sub-Region R83-116W: Calgary, Tijuana, Chur

SUN: Now the versed R83.

EARTH: Yes, the sub-region R83 will have the capitals in Calgary (Canada), Tijuana (Mexico), and Chur (Switzerland). This sub-region R83 is around meridian (longitude) 116^0 W (117^0 W – 114^0 W), having small areas from the Arctic Ocean, Canada, USA, Mexico, Pacific Ocean, Southern Ocean, and Antarctica.

Switzerland, Geneva, Port Miniature on Lac Léman (372 m elevation) and Jet d'Eau – a large fountain pumping water at 0.5 m^3/s to 140 m.

Sub-Region R84-112W: Hermosillo, Tucson, Bergen

SUN: Ready for the artful R84.

EARTH: Yes, the sub-region R84 will have the capitals in Hermosillo (Mexico), Tucson (AR, USA), and Bergen (Norway). This sub-region R84 is around meridian (longitude) 112^0 W (114^0 W – 110^0 W), having small areas from the Arctic Ocean, Canada, USA, Mexico, Pacific Ocean, Southern Ocean, and Antarctica.

USA, Newport (1639): The east side of Rosecliff, 1898-1902, 2.4 ha, Hermann Oelrichs (1850-1906, shipping) and wife Theresa Fair Oelrichs (1871-1926).

Sub-Region R85-107W: Chihuahua, Regina, Gothenburg

SUN: Now the laudable R85.

EARTH: Yes, the sub-region R85 will have the capitals in Chihuahua (Mexico), Regina (Canada), and Gothenburg (Sweden). This sub-region R85 is around meridian (longitude) 107^0 W (110^0 W – 105^0 W), having small areas from the Arctic Ocean, Canada, USA, Mexico, Pacific Ocean, Southern Ocean, and Antarctica.

The Rainbow Bridge between Canada (left) and USA (right), crosses Niagara River, 500 m north-west from the American Falls, opened 1941, longest span 298 m, seen from the Prospect Point Observation Tower (70 m north of the American Falls).

Sub-Region R86-102W: San Luis Potosi City, Winnipeg, Yverdon-les-Bains

SUN: The superlative R86 comes next.

EARTH: Yes, the sub-region R86 will have the capitals in San Luis Potosi City (Mexico), Winnipeg (Canada), and Yverdon-les-Bains (Switzerland).
This sub-region R86 is around meridian (longitude) 102^0 W (105^0 W – 100^0 W), having small areas from the Arctic Ocean, Canada, USA, Mexico, Pacific Ocean, Southern Ocean, and Antarctica.

Switzerland, Geneva (121 BC under Romans, 375 m elevation), Quai Gustave Ador at Rue du 31 Décember (right), from the road to the Jet d'Eau.

Sub-Region R87-95W: Tulsa, Veracruz, Bregenz

SUN: Now the imposing R87.

EARTH: Yes, the sub-region R87 will have the capitals in Tulsa (OK, USA), Veracruz (Mexico), and Bregenz (Austria). This sub-region R87 is around meridian (longitude) 95^0 W (100^0 W $- 90^0$ W), having small areas from the Arctic Ocean, Canada, USA, Mexico, Pacific Ocean, Southern Ocean, and Antarctica.

USA, Newport (1639): The western façade of Marble House, 1888-1892, 50 rooms, 14,000 m^3 of marble, 1.6 ha, William Kissam Vanderbilt (1849-1920, younger brother of Cornelius), and his wife Alva (1853-1933).

Sub-Region R88-85W: Memphis, San José, Uppsala

SUN: Next is the majestic R88.

EARTH: Yes, the sub-region R88 will have the capitals in Memphis (TN, USA), San José (Costa Rica), and Uppsala (Sweden).

This sub-region R88 is around meridian (longitude) 85^0 W (90^0 W - 80^0 W), having small areas from the Arctic Ocean, Canada, USA, Honduras, Nicaragua, Costa Rica, Pacific Ocean, Southern Ocean, and Antarctica.

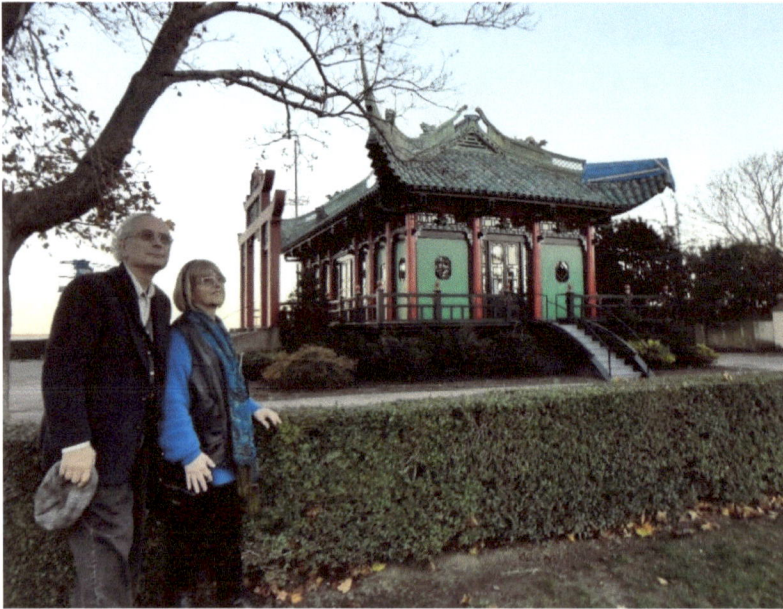

USA, Newport (1639): The Chinese Tea House (1150 Song Dynasty temple style) on the eastern end, near the ocean, of the backyard of Marble House, 1888-1892, William Kissam Vanderbilt (1849-1920), and his wife Alva.

Sub-Region R89-75W: Lima, Boston, Tampere

SUN: Finally, the glorious R89.

EARTH: Yes, the sub-region R89 will have the capitals in Lima (Peru), Boston (MA, USA), and Tampere (Finland).
This sub-region R89 is around meridian (longitude) 75^0 W (80^0 W - 70^0 W), having small areas from the Arctic Ocean, Canada, USA, Bahamas, Cuba, Colombia, Peru, Chile, Pacific Ocean, Southern Ocean, and Antarctica.

Boston Harbor (1614, 130 km^2): east of Rowes Wharf bldg (1987; in 1666 was a battery, in 1764 John Rowe built the first wharf).

10 - Region R9: 70W – 0: Halifax, Brasilia, Biel

SUN: Let's see now the 10th and last grand region R9.

EARTH: Yes, R9 is defined between meridians here 70^0 W and 0, with capitals in Halifax (Canada), Brasilia (Brazil), and Biel (Switzerland).

SUN: This last 10th region R9 covers the eastern parts of the Americas, a good part of the western Atlantic and parts of the western Europe and Africa. We know both meridians.

EARTH: Yes, we have now a region which includes most of South America, the Atlantic Ocean, and western parts of Europe and Africa.

Switzerland, Geneva (121 BC under Romans, 375 m elevation), Quai Gustave Ador at Rue du 31 Décember (left), from the road to the Jet d'Eau.

Sub-Region R90- 68W: La Paz, Bangor, Aosta

SUN: Good, let's start now with the first if its 10 stately sub-regions, R90.

EARTH: Yes, the sub-region R90 will have the capitals in La Paz (Bolivia), Bangor (Maine, USA), and Aosta (Italy).
This sub-region R90 is around meridian (longitude) 68^0 W (70^0 W - 66^0 W), having small areas from the Arctic Ocean, Canada, Greenland, USA, Venezuela, Colombia, Brazil, Bolivia, Chile, Argentina, Pacific Ocean, Southern Ocean, and Antarctica.

France, Chamonix, entrance from France in Mont Blank tunnel (1959-1965, 11.6 km, 8.6 m by 4.35 m, elevation 1274 m) on 21 Oct 2015, 9:43 AM. The highway tunnel links Chamonix, Haute-Savoie, France with Courmayeur, Aosta Valley, Italy, via European route E25.

Sub-Region R91-64W Caracas, Road Town, Obergoms

SUN: Now the palatial R91.

EARTH: Yes, the sub-region R91 will have the capitals in Caracas (Venezuela), Road Town (British Virgin Islands), and Obergoms (Switzerland).

This sub-region R91 is around meridian (longitude) 64^0 W (66^0 W - 62^0 W), having small areas from the Arctic Ocean, Canada, Greenland, Venezuela, Brazil, Bolivia, Argentina, Atlantic Ocean, Southern Ocean, and Antarctica.

Switzerland, Lausanne (150), Place de la Navigation, the south side of Hotel Aulac in a Belle Époque-style building, Château d'Ouchy (right).

Sub-Region R92-60W: Buenos Aires, Fort-de-France, Freudenstadt

SUN: Ready for the admirable R92.

EARTH: Yes, the sub-region R92 will have the capitals in Buenos Aires (Argentina), Fort-de-France (Martinique), and Freudenstadt (Germany).

This sub-region R92 is around meridian (longitude) 60^0 W (62^0 W - 58^0 W), having small areas from the Arctic Ocean, Greenland, Canada, Venezuela, Guyana, Brazil, Bolivia, Paraguay, Argentina, Falkland Islands, Atlantic Ocean, Southern Ocean, and Antarctica.

France, Paris, The Panthéon (1758 - 1790, 83 m height, mausoleum in the Latin Quarter in Paris, modeled on the Pantheon (126 AD) in Rome), seen from Rue Soufflot.

Sub-Region R93-56W: Asuncion, Montevideo, Winterthur

SUN: Now the thrilling R93.

EARTH: Yes, the sub-region R93 will have the capitals in Asuncion (Paraguay), Montevideo (Uruguay), and Winterthur (Switzerland).
This sub-region R93 is around meridian (longitude) 56^0 W (58^0 W - 54^0 W), having small areas from the Arctic Ocean, Greenland, Canada, Suriname, Brazil, Paraguay, Argentina, Uruguay, Atlantic Ocean, Southern Ocean, and Antarctica.

Switzerland, Lausanne, playing chess in Place de la Navigation, marina back.

Sub-Region R94-53W: Cayenne, St. John's, Novara

SUN: Next the incredible R94.

EARTH: Yes, the sub-region R94 will have the capitals in Cayenne (French Guiana), St. John's (Canada), and Novara (Italy). This sub-region R94 is around meridian (longitude) 53^0 W (54^0 W - 48^0 W), having small areas from the Arctic Ocean, Greenland, Canada, French Guiana, Brazil, Atlantic Ocean, Southern Ocean, and Antarctica.

Italy, Venezia, Piazza San Marco with Palazzo Ducale (right), Libreria Sansoviniana (next to Palazzo Ducale), Basilica di San Marco (back), Giardini Reali and Il Campanile (center-right), Procuratie Nuove (center to left), Capitano di Porto (left).

Sub-Region R95-35W: Rio de Janeiro, Dakar, Toyama

SUN: Now the super R95, which connects eastern South America with Western Africa.

EARTH: Yes, the sub-region R95 will have the capitals in Rio de Janeiro (Brazil), Dakar (Senegal), and Toyama (Japan).
This sub-region R95 is from meridian (longitude) 48^0 W to 15^0 W having some areas from the Arctic Ocean, Greenland, Iceland, Brazil, Atlantic Ocean, Western Sahara, Mauritania, Senegal, Gambia, Guinea-Bissau, Guinea, Southern Ocean, and Antarctica.

Japan, Inzai Post Office, 300 m north-est from the entrance to the Inzai (Chiba) campus of Tokyo Denki University (TDU, founded in 1907) in Muzai-Gakuendai, 34 km north-east of Tokyo.

Sub-Region R96-12W: Freetown, Lisbon, Kawasaki

SUN: The captivating R96 is waiting.

EARTH: Yes, the sub-region R96 will have the capitals in Freetown (Sierra Leone), Lisbon (Portugal), and Kawasaki (Japan) This sub-region R96 is around meridian (longitude) 12^0 W (15^0 W - 9^0 W) having some areas from the Arctic Ocean, Greenland, Atlantic Ocean, West Sahara, Mauritania, Mali, Senegal, Guinea, Sierra Leone, Southern Ocean, and Antarctica.

Japan, Tsukuba: Photographs and computer presentations at the High Energy Accelerator Research Organization (KEK, 1997) in Tsukuba Science City (1962), in Ibaraki, 60 km north-east of Tokyo.

Sub-Region R97-8W: Bamako, Athlone, Ulm

SUN: Now the wondrous R97.

EARTH: Yes, the sub-region R97 will have the capitals in Bamako (Mali), Athlone (Ireland), and Ulm (Germany)
This sub-region R97 is around meridian (longitude) 8^0 W (9^0 W - 7^0 W) having some areas from the Arctic Ocean, Norway, Atlantic Ocean, Ireland, United Kingdom, Spain, Portugal, Morocco, Algeria, Mauritania, Mali, Guinea, Ivory Coast, Liberia, Southern Ocean, and Antarctica.

UK, London: From the Tower Millennium Pier (right down) looking southeast to Tower Bridge (1894, 244 m, 65 m height, clearance 8.6 m closed).

Sub-Region R98-5W: Yamoussoukro, Madrid, Okayama

SUN: Let's see the radiant R98.

EARTH: Yes, the sub-region R98 will have the capitals in Yamoussoukro (Cote d'Ivoire), Madrid (Spain), and Okayama (Japan).

This sub-region R98 is around meridian (longitude) 5^0 W (7^0 W - 4^0 W) having some areas from the Arctic Ocean, Atlantic Ocean, United Kingdom, Spain, Morocco, Algeria, Mauritania, Mali, Burkina Faso, Guinea, Ivory Coast, Southern Ocean, and Antarctica.

Japan, Kobe, 16 April 2015, the south side of the Kobe Port Tower (1963, 108 m, 90 m deck) and new buildings to the west (left).

Sub-Region R99-2W: Ouagadougou, London, Vaasa

SUN: The last magnificent sub-region R99.

EARTH: Yes, the sub-region R99 will have the capitals in Ouagadougou (Burkina Faso), London (United Kingdom), and Vaasa (Finland).

This sub-region R99 is around meridian (longitude) 2^0 W (4^0 W - 0^0) having some areas from the Arctic Ocean, Atlantic Ocean, United Kingdom, France, Spain, Algeria, Morocco, Mali, Burkina Faso, Ghana, Southern Ocean, and Antarctica.

UK, London: The southeast entrance of The British Museum (1753), exhibition "Sunken cities, Egypt's lost worlds", 19 May – 27 Nov 2016.

UK, Greenwich: At the Royal Observatory Greenwich (1676), the official Greenwich Mean Time (GMT was replaced by Coordinated Universal Time (UTC) in 1960) on the Shepherd 24-hour gate galvano-magnetic clock (10:21:42), public standards of length for British yard (0.9144 m), two feet (0.6096 m), one foot (0.3048 m), six inches (0.1524 m) , three inches (0.0762 m, down), height above mean sea level 154.7 feet (47.15 m, on the plaque in the center up).

11 - Conclusions

SUN: Really good administrative organization of the happy country Terra!

EARTH: Thank you – there are many discrepancies between regions, and between sub-regions, but every 5 years, after census, modifications will take place, for homogenization.

SUN: Will be these homogenizations difficult?

EARTH: Not at all – in fact only the people, who are in the modified areas, will receive from their local government their new special credit cards, which will show the new sub-region or region in which they are now located.

SUN: Like always, there will be differences between different parts of the country Terra.

EARTH: Yes, like in any family, there are differences, and, like in any good family, constant calm and friendly efforts will be done to smooth the differences, and to bring everybody to a better level, in harmony with others. The results will be astonishing!

France, Paris: On la Seine, on a boat, looking upstream, northeast, to the left bank (right): Port de Grenelle (right), Vedettes de Paris Croisières (center), near Quai de Grenelle, the southwest side of la Tour Eiffel (1889, 324 m), Île aux Cygnes (left). Pont de Bir-Hakeim (1905).

World Constitution

SUN: Then a world constitution would be useful.

EARTH: Yes, and we have it in Michael M. Dediu's book "Our Future is Sustainable Peace and Prosperity – Moving from conflicts to harmony and peace"

The following are the main World Constitution subjects:
- limited number of rules
- small World Government, with 7 small departments
- elections - every 20 months for one term only, based on exceptional results, no propaganda
- advisors' levels - minimum age 25 years, First Adviser for one month, by rotation
- assistants
- administrators
- Honorific Word Observer
- medical assistance, Specialized Medical Institutions for disorderly behavior
- people assistance services
- some police with small arms
- total disarmament
- no conflicts
- no war
- no military forces
- no arms
- no abuses
- freedom and responsibility
- people can assemble peacefully only
- census: **A census will take place every 5 years – starting, let's say on October 1st, 2023 - and all the people will receive a special credit card (SCC), with their photo and other personal data.**
- special credit card **with photo and other personal data. The special credit card (SCC) will be used to buy everything, to identify for voting, for census, for travel, for medical assistance, etc.**

    - World Central Bank: **The SCC will be issued by the World Central Bank, which will include all current central banks – starting, let's say on May 1st, 2023.**
    - new world currency
    - budgets with surplus
    - tax: 15% of income
    - no borrowing
    - 40 hours/week, compensation
    - savings accounts for old age
    - International standards
    - Intellectual Property
    - World Post Offices
    - free commerce and collaboration
    - common sense
    - prevention of bad events first - if bad, then pay all expense and reimburse
    - language and alphabet

Japan, Kobe, 16 April 2015, from Kobe Port Tower (1963, 108 m hyperboloid, 90 m deck) looking southeast: Meriken Park (left down), Kobe Meriken Park Oriental Hotel (left center), the west part of the port of Kobe (right) in Osaka Bay, on the west shore of the Pacific Ocean.

Good Managers

SUN: Great! Do you happen to also have some examples of good managers?

EARTH: But of course!

- Jeff Bezos, $131 B, U.S., started Amazon in his garage in 1994, and now he is the richest man in the world. He allocates $1 billion a year to space travel.

- Bill Gates, $96.5 B, U.S., Microsoft co-founder.

- Warren Buffett, $82.5, U.S., Berkshire Hathaway CEO.

- Bernard Arnault, $76 B, French billionaire who owns LVMH, parent company to brands such as Louis Vuitton and Sephora. He is the richest man in Europe.

- Amancio Ortega, 83, $69.7 B, Spain, the cofounder of Inditex, the conglomerate which owns clothing giant Zara; he is the richest retailer in the world.

- Carlos Slim Helú, $64, Mexico, is the head of telecom company América Móvil, making him the richest man in Latin America. He also has investments in construction, real estate and mining.

- Larry Ellison, $62.5, U. S., Oracle cofounder.

- Larry Page, $50.8 B, U.S. is the Google cofounder.

- Charles Koch, $50.5, U.S. has headed up Koch Industries since 1967.

- Mukesh Ambani, $50 B, India, inherited Reliance Industries from his father, Dhirubhai Ambani. The oil and gas company now has revenues of $90 B, meaning Ambani is the richest man in Asia.

Italy: 3 Nov 2009, on the left bank of the Natisone River (flowing from right to left), at the southeast end of the bridge of Iacopo da Bissone (1442, 50 m by 3.6 m, height 22.5 m, rock), 200 m southeast of Palazzo Comunale, looking northwest to the northeast side of the bridge and the right bank of the river, with il Campanile (up right) of il Duomo di Santa Maria Assunta (1457-1529).

- Sergey Brin, $49.8 B, U.S., the cofounder of Google, heads up Google's parent company Alphabet, and also ran Google X.

- Jim Walton, $44.6 B, U. S., the youngest son of Walmart founder Sam Walton

- Rob Walton, $44.3 B, U. S., the eldest son of Walmart founder Sam Walton.

- Steve Ballmer, $41.2, U.S., is a businessman and investor who became a billionaire because of the stock he received as CEO of Microsoft from 2000 to 2014.

- Ma Huateng, $38.8 B, co-founded internet company Tencent in 1998, and is China's richest man.

- Jack Ma, $37.3 B, China, cofounder of the hugely successful e-commerce giant Alibaba Group.

- Phil Knight, 81, $36.6 B, U.S., owes much of his wealth to sportswear giant Nike, which he founded in 1964.

- Hui Ka Yan, $36.2, China, is chairman of real estate development empire the Evergrande Group.

- Sheldon Adelson, $35.1 B, U. S., is the CEO of casino chain Las Vegas Sands

- Michael Dell, $34.3 B, is the CEO of Dell Technologies, although most of his wealth comes from his investments in commercial property.

- David Thomson, $32.5 B, is the richest man in Canada. His wealth comes from the publishing empire built by his grandfather Roy, which includes Thomson Reuters.

Japan, Kobe, 16 April 2015, Hotel Piena Kobe, with Italian style furnishings in 90 rooms, a breakfast buffet with fish from Awaji Island and all-you-can-eat sweets at an excellent patisserie, French and Italian cuisine at a Kobe-style restaurant, and Milkish Jam (a specialty handmade milk jam, can be purchased at Kashi's Patrie). Located 800 m south of Shin-Kobe Station, 600 m north of Sannomiya Station, 100 m east of the Flower Road, 150 m west of Ninomiya Shrine, 800 m northeast of Ikuta Shrine, and 250 m east of Ichinomiya Shrine.

- Li Ka-shing, $31.7, China, one of the most successful entrepreneurs in Asia. Li retired in 2018, but still acts as senior adviser to CK Hutchison Holdings and CK Asset Holdings, two conglomerates with multiple investments.

- Lee Shau-kee, 91, $30.1, Hong Kong, came from humble beginnings. He founded Henderson Land Development in 1976, and also co-owns property development firm Sun Hung Kai.

- François Pinault, $29.7 B, France, built and chairs the Kering Group. Founded in 1963, it began life as a building supplies company, and now owns fashion houses including Gucci and Alexander McQueen.

- Joseph Safra, 81, $24.7, Brazil, born in Aleppo, Syria, is the world's richest banker.

- Leonid Mikhelson, $24 B, Russia, built and chairs natural gas company Novatek. He is the richest man in Russia.

- John Mars, $23.9 B, U.K., inherited his fortune from the family's confectionery business when his father died in 1999. Mars Inc. was founded in 1911 by John's grandfather, Frank.

- Jorge Paulo Lemann, $22.8, Brazil, made his fortune through investment banking, and then as a shareholder of brewing giant Anheuser-Busch InBev. He is a co-founder of investment group 3G Capital, which joined forces with Warren Buffett's Berkshire Hathaway in 2013 in order to acquire the H. J. Heinz Co. for $28 B.

- Dieter Schwarz, $22.6 B, Germany, from his father Josef, who founded Schwarz Gruppe, which owns supermarket chain Lidl.

- Wang Jianlin, $22.6 B, China, is chairman of Dalian Wanda Group, China's largest real estate developer, which has a massive commercial property portfolio, including 260 plazas across China. In 2017 he sold his China hotel and tourism empire for $9 B.

USA, the University of California, Berkeley (1868, named after the philosopher and mathematician Bishop George Berkeley (1685-1753), 19 December 2014, motto Fiat lux (Let there be light), 36,200 students, 72 Nobel laureates, il Campanile (Sather Tower (61 bells (full concert carillon) and clock tower). 1914, 94 m, 7 floors, observation deck - 8th floor, inspired by il Campanile (850, 1514, 1912, 99 m) di San Marco (1084), Venezia (421), Italy (900 BC)).

- Azim Premji, $22.6, India, dropped out of Stanford University in 1966 in order to head up the family business after the death of his father. After Premji shifted the cooking oil enterprise into the software industry, the company, renamed Wipro, became extremely lucrative.

- Giovanni Ferrero, $22.4 B, Italy, heads up the family's Ferrero confectionery empire. He acquired U.K. chocolatier Thorntons for $140 millions in 2015, the Ferrara Candy Co. for $1.3 B in 2017 and Nestle's American confectionery business for $2.8 B in 2018. In April it was announced that the Ferrero Group would also purchase multiple well-known brands from Kellogg for $1.3 B.

- Tadashi Yanai, $22.2 B, the richest man in Japan, founded and runs the Fast Retailing fashion group, which owns Uniqlo. The billionaire is aiming to overtake Inditex, and become the world's biggest retailer

- Vagit Alekperov, 69, $22 B, the president of the leading Russian oil company LUKOIL.

- Masayoshi Son, $21.6 B, Japanese founder and CEO of investment firm SoftBank. The company's investment arm, the Vision Fund, is the biggest tech fund in history, and has made investments in Uber, WeWork, Yahoo Japan, Slack and Brightstar. The Japanese billionaire

- James Simons, retired, $21.5 B, U.S., found Renaissance Technologies in 1982. The hedge fund currently manages more than $110 B.

- Vladimir Lisin, $21.3 B, Russian chairman of metals manufacturer NLMK

12 April 2015, impressive buildings after Mikawa-Anjo Station and before Nagoya (started with the Great Atsuta Shrine, 100 AD, now the fourth most populous area in Japan, the capital of Aichi Prefecture, one of Japan's major ports on the Pacific Ocean, its Chubu Centrair International Airport is built on an artificial island in Tokoname, and Nagoya Station is the world's largest train station by floor area), seen from a Shinkansen (new trunk line) – a bullet train (300 km/h) from Shin Fuji Station to Kyoto.

Pour la bon bouche

SUN: Now, pour la bon bouche, what you have to say?

EARTH: - Let's start with children - if all over 2 billions of children in the world will get a solid peace-oriented education (see Dediu's book at number 90 in bibliography: Our Future Depends on Good World Educations – Moving from frail education to solid education), our future will be in good hands!

SUN: What is the purpose of education?

EARTH: Simply, to give a solid peace-oriented foundation for a good, free, peaceful and prosperous life.

SUN: What is the advantage of this longitudinal administrative organization?

EARTH: Having telework, many people will have a northern residence and a southern residence, seasonally moving from one to the other, to avoid extreme cold or heat, and having the same hour.

SUN: Now tell me, what is the purpose for all over 7.7 billions of people on Earth?

EARTH: Good question: it is to be healthy, to live in peace, freedom and harmony, to be prosperous, and to prepare to expand to the Moon, asteroids, Mars, and other places in the Universe, which can support life.

SUN: I see, you want them to go to my other planets and asteroids, and even out of my Solar system! That's great! And what ideas do you have for their future?

EARTH: First of all, they must have a good World Government, as described in Dediu's book "Friendly, Helpful &

Smart World Management - Moving from bureaucracy to responsive world management". Then they will do the following:
- Reserve time for happiness
- Use robots and automated processes, work less, and spend more time with their families
- The weekend will be like a small vacation
- Prevent burnout
- Make civilized harmony everywhere an important issue
- Eliminate stress
- Help friends and colleagues
- Having telework, many people will have a northern residence and a southern residence, seasonally moving from one to the other, to avoid extreme cold or heat.
- Keep everybody relaxed, calm, friendly, patient, and happy.

SUN: Excellent! That's the way to go, and I wish you all good health and great success!

EARTH: Thank you, Sun, and please continue to send us your energy, light, and so many other good things, without which we cannot live.

SUN: I cannot refuse you; you'll have them all, and enjoy the Sun in all your 10 lovely regions!

Italy, Venezia: Palazzo Querini (right), Canale di Cannaregio (center-right), Palazzo Labia (center-right), Chiesa San Geremia (center-left), 350 m east from the Venice Santa Lucia Train Station, 1.3 km from the west end of the Canal, and 2.6 km from Piazza San Marco.

Bibliography

"The Histories" by Polybius
"Discours de la Méthode" by René Descartes
"Meditationes de prima philosophia" by René Descartes
"Philosophiae Naturalis Principia Mathematica" by Isaac Newton
Chinese encyclopedia Gujin Tushu Jicheng (Imperial Enciclopaedia)
"Encyclopédie" by Jean-Baptiste le Rond d'Alembert and Denis Diderot
"Encyclopaedia Britannica" by over 4,400 contributors
"Encyclopedia Americana" by Francis Lieber
"Grand Larousse encyclopédique en 24 volumes" by Albert Ducrocq
Nobel Prize Organization
"The Cambridge History of Medicine", edited by Roy Porter
"Great Russian Encyclopedia" by Yury Osipov
"Encyclopedia of China"
"Enciclopedia Italiana di Scienze, Lettere ed Arti" (35 volume), by Giovanni Treccani
Concise Oxford Dictionary of Opera
"Allgemeine Encyclopädie der Wissenschaften und Künste" by Johann Samuel Ersch und Johann Gottfried Gruber
Grove Dictionary of Music and Musicians
"Gran Enciclopedia de España"
Other sources include: UPI, CNBC, AP, Nasdaq, Reuters, EDGAR, AFP, Recode, Europa Press, Bloomberg News, Fox News, USA, Deutsche Presse-Agentur, MSNBC, BBC, Australian Associated Press, Agência Brasil, The Canadian Press (La Presse Canadienne), Middle East News Agency, Baltic News Service, Suomen Tietotoimisto, Athens-Macedonian News Agency, Asian News International, Inter Press Service, Kyodo News, Notimex, Algemeen Nederlands Persbureau, AGERPRES, Newsis, Tidningarnas Telegrambyrå, Swiss Telegraphic Agency, Central News Agency, ANKA news agency, Agenzia Fides

Italy: 3 Nov 2009, on Via Nicolo Lionello, just southwest of Loggia del Lionello, looking east to the southwest façade of the Palazzo di Comune di Udine (City Hall).

Michael M. Dediu is also the author of these books (which can be found on Amazon.com):

1. Aphorisms and quotations – with examples and explanations
2. Axioms, aphorisms and quotations – with examples and explanations
3. 100 Great Personalities and their Quotations
4. Professor Petre P. Teodorescu – A Great Mathematician and Engineer
5. Professor Ioan Goia – A Dedicated Engineering Professor
6. Venice (Venezia) – a new perspective. A short presentation with photographs
7. La Serenissima (Venice) - a new photographic perspective. A short presentation with many photos
8. Grand Canal – Venice. A new photographic viewpoint. A short presentation with many photos
9. Piazza San Marco – Venice. A different photographic view. A short presentation with many photos
10. Roma (Rome) - La Città Eterna. A new photographic view. A short presentation with many photos
11. Why is Rome so Fascinating? A short presentation with many photos
12. Rome, Boston and Helsinki. A short photographic presentation
13. Rome and Tokyo – two captivating cities. A short photographic presentation
14. Beautiful Places on Earth – A new photographic presentation
15. From Niagara Falls to Mount Fuji via Rome - A novel photographic presentation
16. From the USA and Canada to Italy and Japan - A fresh photographic presentation
17. Paris – Why So Many Call This City Mon Amour - A lovely photographic presentation
18. The City of Light – Paris (La Ville-Lumière) - A kaleidoscopic photographic presentation
19. Paris (Lutetia Parisiorum) – the romance capital of the world - A kaleidoscopic photographic view
20. Paris and Tokyo – a joyful photographic presentation. With a preamble about the Universe

Italy, Venezia, Il Torre dell'Orologio (the Clock Tower) is on the north side of the Piazza San Marco (1499). On the top of the Torre there are two big bronze statues, hinged at the waist, which strike the hours on the bell. One is old and the other young and they are wearing sheepskins. The Winged Lion of Venice is below the bell and holds the book quoting "Pax Tibi Marce Evangelista Meus" (Peace to you Mark my evangelist).

21. From USA to Japan via Canada – A cheerful photographic documentary

22. 200 Wonderful Places, In The Last 50 Years – A personal photographic documentary

23. Must see places in USA and Japan - A kaleidoscopic photographic documentary

24. Grandeurs of the World - A kaleidoscopic photographic documentary

25. Corneliu Leu – writer on the same wavelength as Mark Twain. An American viewpoint

26. From Berkeley to Pompeii via Rome – A kaleidoscopic photographic documentary

27. From America to Europe via Japan - A kaleidoscopic photographic documentary

28. Discover America and Japan - A photographic documentary

29. J. R. Lucas – philosopher on a creative parallel with Plato, An American viewpoint

30. From America to Switzerland via France - A photographic documentary

31. From Bretton Woods to New York via Cape Cod - A photographic documentary

32. Splendid Places on the Atlantic Coast of the U. S. A. - A photographic documentary

33. Fourteen nice Cities on three Continents - A photographic documentary

34. 17 Picturesque Cities on the World Map - A photographic documentary

35. Unforgettable Places from Four Continents including Trump buildings - A photographic documentary

36. Dediu Newsletter, Volume 1, Number 1, 6 December 2016 – Monthly news, review, comments and suggestions for a better and wiser world

37. Dediu Newsletter, Volume 1, Number 2, 6 January 2017 (available at www.derc.com).

38. Dediu Newsletter, Volume 1, Number 3, 6 February 2017 (available at www.derc.com).

39. London and Greenwich, A photographic documentary

A beautiful tall ship on the north-west side of the Boston Fish Pier. Bostonians welcome tall ships and their crews and cadets, from all over the world, to their harbor, on a continuous basis.

40. Dediu Newsletter, Volume 1, Number 4, 6 March 2017 (available also at www.derc.com).

41. Dediu Newsletter, Volume 1, Number 5, 6 April 2017 (available also at www.derc.com).

42. Dediu Newsletter, Volume 1, Number 6, 6 May 2017 (available also at www.derc.com).

43. Dediu Newsletter, Volume 1, Number 7, 6 June 2017 (available also at www.derc.com).

44. London, Oxford and Cambridge, A photographic documentary

45. Dediu Newsletter, Volume 1, Number 8, 6 July 2017 (available also at www.derc.com).

46. Dediu Newsletter, Volume 1, Number 9, 6 August 2017 (available also at www.derc.com).

47. Dediu Newsletter, Volume 1, Number 10, 6 September 2017 (available also at www.derc.com).

48. Three Great Professors: President Woodrow Wilson, Historian Germán Arciniegas, Mathematician Gheorghe Vrănceanu, A chronological and photographic documentary

49. Dediu Newsletter, Volume 1, Number 11, 6 October 2017 (available also at www.derc.com).

50 Dediu Newsletter, Volume 1, Number 12, 6 November 2017 (available also at www.derc.com).

51 Dediu Newsletter, Volume 2, Number 1 (13), 6 December 2017 (available also at www.derc.com).

52 Two Great Leaders: Augustus and George Washington, A chronological and photographic documentary

53. Dediu Newsletter, Volume 2, Number 2 (14), 6 January 2018 (available also at www.derc.com).

54. Newton, Benjamin Franklin, and Gauss, A chronological and photographic documentary

55. Dediu Newsletter, Volume 2, Number 3 (15), 6 February 2018 (available also at www.derc.com).

56. 2017: World Top Events, But Many Little Known, A chronological and photographic documentary

57. Dediu Newsletter, Volume 2, Number 4 (16), 6 March 2018 (available also at www.derc.com).

58. Vergilius, Horatius, Ovidius, and Shakespeare, A chronological and photographic documentary.

Finland, Helsinki: This imposing building is at the south-east end of
the Stockmann department store, located in the center of Helsinki,
near Esplanadi.

59. Dediu Newsletter, Volume 2, Number 5 (17), 6 April 2018 (available also at www.derc.com).

60. Dediu Newsletter, Volume 2, Number 6 (18), 6 May 2018 (available also at www.derc.com).

61. Vivaldi, Bach, Mozart, and Verdi, A chronological and photographic documentary

62. Dediu Newsletter, Volume 2, Number 7 (19), 6 June 2018 (available also at www.derc.com).

63. Dediu Newsletter, Volume 2, Number 8 (20), 6 July 2018 (available also at www.derc.com).

64. Dediu Newsletter, Volume 2, Number 9 (21), 6 August 2018 (available also at www.derc.com).

65. World History, a new perspective - A chronological and photographic documentary.

66. World Humor History with over 100 Jokes, a new perspective - A chronological and photographic documentary

67. Dediu Newsletter, Vol 2, N 10 (22), 6 September 2018

68. Dediu Newsletter, Vol 2, N 11 (23), 6 October 2018

69. Da Vinci, Michelangelo, Rembrandt, Rodin - A chronological and photographic documentary

70. Dediu Newsletter, Vol 2, N 12 (24), 6 November 2018

71. Dediu Newsletter, Vol 3, N 1 (25), 6 December 2018

72. From Euclid to Edison - revelries in the last 75 years - A chronological and photographic documentary

73. Dediu Newsletter, Vol 3, N 2 (26), 6 January 2019

74. Socrates to Churchill - Aphorisms celebrated after 1960 - A chronological and photographic documentary

75. Dediu Newsletter Vol 3, Number 3 (27), 6 February 2019

76. Hippocrates to Fleming: Medicine History celebrated after 1943 - A chronological and photographic documentary

77. Dediu Newsletter, Volume 3, Number 4 (28), 6 March 2019

78. Dediu Newsletter, Volume 3, Number 5 (29), 6 April 2019

79. Archimedes to Ford: Invention History celebrated after 1943 - A chronological and photographic documentary

80. Dediu Newsletter, Volume 3, Number 6 (30), 6 May 2019

81. Sutherland to Pavarotti: Great Singers History - A chronological and photographic documentary

82. Dediu Newsletter, Volume 3, Number 7 (31), 6 June 2019

83. Dediu Newsletter, Volume 3, Number 8 (32), 6 July 2019

84. Augustus to Rockefeller: History of the Wealthiest People - A chronological and photographic documentary
85. Dediu Newsletter, Volume 3, Number 9 (33), 6 August 2019
86 – Pythagoras to Fermi: History of Science - A chronological and photographic documentary
87. Dediu Newsletter, Volume 3, Number 10 (34), 6 September 2019
88. Our Future is Sustainable Peace and Prosperity – Moving from conflicts to harmony and peace
89 - Dediu Newsletter, Volume 3, Number 11 (35), 6 October 2019 – World Monthly Report with News
90 – Our Future Depends on Good World Educations – Moving from frail education to solid education
91 - Dediu Newsletter, Volume 3, Number 12 (36), 6 November 2019 – World Monthly Report with News
92 – Friendly, Helpful & Smart World Management - Moving from bureaucracy to responsive world management
93 – If You Want Peace, Prepare for Peace! – Moving from preparation for war to preparation for peace
94 - Dediu Newsletter, Volume 4, Number 1 (37), 6 December 2019 – World Monthly Report with News

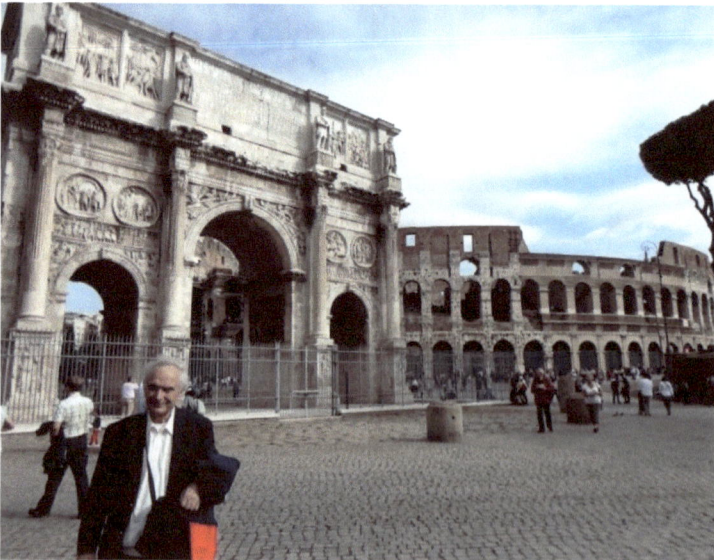

Italy, Rome: The south side of Arch of Constantine (315, left), and the south-west side of Amphitheatrum Flavium (Colosseum, 80 AD)

Michael M. Dediu is the editor of these books (also on Amazon.com):

1. Sophia Dediu: The life and its torrents – Ana. In Europe around 1920
2. Proceedings of the 4th International Conference "Advanced Composite Materials Engineering" COMAT 2012
3. Adolf Shvedchikov: I am an eternal child of spring – poems in English, Italian, French, German, Spanish and Russian
4. Adolf Shvedchikov: Life's Enigma – poems in English, Italian and Russian
5. Adolf Shvedchikov: Everyone wants to be HAPPY – poems in English, Spanish and Russian
6. Adolf Shvedchikov: My Life, My Love – poems in English, Italian and Russian
7. Adolf Shvedchikov: I am the gardener of love – poems in English and Russian
8. Adolf Shvedchikov: Amaretta di Saronno – poems in English and Russian
9. Adolf Shvedchikov: A Russian Rediscovers America
10. Adolf Shvedchikov: Parade of Life - poems in English and Russian
11. Adolf Shvedchikov: Overcoming Sorrow - poems in English and Russian
12. Sophia Dediu: Sophia meets Japan
13. Corneliu Leu: Roosevelt, Churchill, Stalin and Hitler: Their surprising role in Eastern Europe in 1944
14. Proceedings of the 5th International Conference "Computational Mechanics and Virtual Engineering" COMEC 2013
15. Georgeta Simion – Potanga: Beyond Imagination: A Thought-provoking novel inspired from mid-20th century events
16. Ana Dediu: The poetry of my life in Europe and The USA
17. Ana Dediu: The Four Graces
18. Proceedings of the 5th International Conference "Advanced Composite Materials Engineering" COMAT 2014
19. Sophia Dediu: Chocolate Cook Book: Is there such a thing as too much chocolate?

20. Sorin Vlase: Mechanical Identifiability in Automotive Engineering
21. Gabriel Dima: The Evolution of the Aerostructures – Concept and Technologies
22. Proceedings of the 6th International Conference "Computational Mechanics and Virtual Engineering" COMEC 2015
23. Sophia Dediu: Cook Book 1 A-B-C Common sense cooking
24. Sophia Dediu: Dim Sum Spring Festival
25. Ana Dediu and Sophia Dediu: Europe in 1985: A chronological and photographic documentary
26 Stefan Staretu: Europe: Serbian Despotate of Srem and the Romanian area. Between the 14th and the 16th Centuries

USA, California, Berkeley, in a beautiful garden near Claremont Sport.